Curriculum-Based Motivational Group

Developed by

Ann Fields, MA, CADC III, CGAC II
Portland, Oregon
2004

A MODEL FOR BROAD APPLICATION

THIS CURRICULUM – BASED MOTIVATION GROUP MODEL HAS BROAD APPLICATION FOR ALL TREATMENT PROVIDERS, COUNSELORS, THERAPISTS, EDUCATORS AND OTHER HUMAN SERVICE PRACTITIONERS.

IT ALLOWS FOR THE FACILITATION AND IMPLEMENTATION OF MOTIVATIONAL INTERVIEWING STRATEGIES WITHIN **FIVE GROUP SESSIONS.**

THIS GROUP PROCESS AND APPROACH ELICITS AND EFFECTS POSITIVE CHANGE IN THE LIVES OF PEOPLE STRUGGLING WITH LIFE CHOICES AND PERSONAL BEHAVIOR, AFFECTING THEIR OVERALL HEALTH, WELLBEING AND FUNCTIONING.

*Note – Throughout this manual "changing your behavior" can be any behavior / life change (i.e. anger, addictions, leaving an abusive relationship, illegal behaviors, taking medications, and managing health concerns, changing careers and going back to school).

Table of Contents

Acknowledgements

I would like to thank my partner, Mindy Holliday, Program Director / Assistant Professor of the Child Welfare Partnership in the Graduate School of Social Work, at Portland State University, for her ongoing encouragement, inspiration and business ingenuity in assisting me in completing this project. I would also like to thank Nikki Johnson, Director of Daystar Education Associates and Adjunct Faculty at Portland Community College, for her openness as a teacher, her generosity in time and commitment in completing this project and her professional integrity as a trainer, writer and mentor. Both Mindy and Nikki assisted me in taking my vision of this project and making it into a reality. I would also like to thank my family (Jenni, Michael, Robbie, Sarah, Jen, John, Andy, Erin, Allie, John, and Stephanie) for their love and support.

Ann Fields
January, 2004

This document represents Ann Fields' move from practitioner to information disseminator. Ann has used and refined this model through her years of clinical practice. She has trained various groups in the theory and practice of motivational interviewing. In this endeavor she presents in a concrete and explicit way, the structure she uses in her groups.

This document is designed to be a manual for practitioners, with all of the details provided, including the paperwork and logistical tips she has learned through trial and error. It will be most successfully utilized in the context of being trained with the model and receiving this manual as part of the training. We are not naïve enough to think that will always happen. So it is very complete. People with some training and appreciation for motivational interviewing will also readily apply it. But Ann has painstakingly provided the conceptual models for every action taken. People with little background in MI will learn and experience MI if they take the direction provided here.

It has been my pleasure to help Ann put this on paper in a form designed to help train others. For my experience in this project, I saw the articulateness and thoughtfulness that went into each element of the group. Every action was calculated in service to the enhancement of client motivation. Ann has done her homework. Practitioners will benefit and clients will benefit from her contributions to helping people with problem behaviors change.

Finally, this manual, with its use of motivational interviewing, gets counselors back to the basics. This model requires that counselors once again, listen and listen deeply to their clients and use what they hear to motivate change. It is client centered, but it is certainly not non-directive.

Nikki Johnson, MA
Daystar Education Associates

Why design a motivational group?

I took William Miller's first training for trainers in 1993. When I began to utilize a motivational style and motivational strategies with my individual clients, I saw how effecting change was a process. It became clear to me that Motivational Interviewing (MI) could be utilized in a variety of settings with diverse client populations and with diverse needs. I explored research-based conceptual models for understanding motivation and developed exercises to be facilitated with an MI approach. I found these exercises to be revealing, eliciting problem recognition, discrepancies, change talk and affecting the client's process of change.

In 1996 I was working in a gambling addiction agency where clients had weekly individual counseling. As the political climate changed and the budgets cuts greater, group counseling became the primary modality available. It was during this time that I started to explore how I could utilize motivational interviewing strategies in a group format. The research stated MI improved treatment retention by decreasing resistance and enhancing client motivation and commitment for change. I selected the exercises I had designed from the conceptual models for understanding motivation that would effect client movement in the earlier stages of change. I began formulating the rationale for the group, its purpose, and a description of the mindset needed to facilitate a motivational group. What resulted was a five-week group, with sessions lasting one and a half hours, once per week. This was an open group, where new members could join at any time. The group was utilized for clients at various stages of change. The group consisted of 1) clients at the beginning of their treatment, who were not ready for action, and /or for 2) clients in the middle of their treatment, who started out in action, but were showing signs of ambivalence and 3) for clients at the end of their treatment for closure and recommitment to their goals. It became a very powerful group, assisting clients in resolving their ambivalence about change and/or enhancing their intrinsic desire for change.

Conceptual Models For Understanding Motivation: A Review
*How I utilized conceptual models for understanding motivation
in my curriculum and with my clients.*

1. <u>**Stages of Change**</u> – Prochaska & DiClemente's process of change (1991) defined several stages through which people <u>normally</u> pass in the process of changing.

Both counselors and clients need to be educated regarding the stages of change. Counselors need to understand the change process to: 1) normalize where clients are in the process of change and 2) to utilize appropriate strategies to assist clients in moving through the different stages. Clients need to understand the change process to normalize what they may experience related to changing a particular behavior.

CURRICULUM:

- *Session One – Orientation / Pre – Assessment Exercises*: The counselor will educate new clients on the Stages of Change. Clients assess where they are on the change wheel.

- *Session Five – Vision / Post – Assessment Exercises*: The Stages of Change are utilized with clients as a Post – self-assessment exercise to compare with their Pre-self-assessment exercise they completed in Session One. During this time clients are able to identify their movement in the change process, as forward, backward, or the same.

2. <u>**Conflict – ambivalence**</u> – In conflict situations, ambivalence is a normal, defining condition of the stage of contemplation, and is a key obstacle to change.

Both counselors and clients need to understand that feeling two ways about changing a behavior is normal. It is up to counselors to assist clients in clarifying and resolving their ambivalence through the use of appropriate strategies. Ambivalence is not resistance.

CURRICULUM:

- *Session One - Orientation*: The counselor will normalize ambivalence when he/she is educating clients about the stage of contemplation in the wheel of change.

- *Session Three - Pros & Cons*: The counselor will also facilitate clients in weighing both sides of their ambivalence, related to the costs and benefits of their behavior.

3. <u>**Health Beliefs Model**</u> – Ronald Rogers Protection Theory (1976) states motivation for change depends upon the presence of a sufficient degree of perceived risks, in combination with sufficient self-efficacy.

Both counselors and clients need to understand that for change to occur, clients need to: 1) become aware of the possibility of risks and/or the severity of risks, if they continue to engage in a particular behavior and 2) their degree of self-efficacy. If clients have low self-efficacy, their belief that change is possible will be low. Counselors need to utilize appropriate strategies to increase clients' awareness of risks and assess clients' degree of self-efficacy, for change to occur.

CURRICULUM:

- **Session One – Orientation / Pre-Assessment Exercises:** *The counselor educates clients about the importance of becoming aware of risks and self-efficacy, when discussing the process of moving from contemplation to preparation in the Stages of Change. The counselor also provides clients with two self-assessment exercises to raise their awareness of risks and rate their degree of self-efficacy: 1)* **Areas of Impact** *– To assess the degree of impact their particular behavior has had on the different areas of their lives. 2)* **Commitment / Confidence Rating** *– To rate their commitment level to change their behavior and rate their confidence level, that they have the skills to change their behavior.*

- **Session Two – Feelings Exercise 2:** *Clients become aware of their feelings related to the different areas of their lives that have been impacted by their behavior.*

- **Session Three – Pros & Cons Exercise:** *Clients become aware of the pros and cons of their behavior. Clients identify and clarify their short-term pros. The counselor assists clients in identifying and clarifying ways they have successfully avoided and/or altered their short-term pros. The counselor also addresses client's degree of self-efficacy by affirming and reflecting what has worked and by providing additional options and choices.*

4. <u>**Decisional Balance**</u> – Janis & Mann (1977). Decision is a process of weighing the pros & cons of change cognitively.

Counselors need to assist their clients in weighing out the short and long term pros and cons of continuing their behavior. This helps clients clarify and assess their need for change. They weigh the different factors that do or do not support their behavior. With the use of appropriate MI strategies, this problem-solving skill can allow for decision-making that leans toward change, based on clients' own arguments for change.

CURRICULUM:

- **Session Three – Pros & Cons:** *The counselor will ask the group to brainstorm the short and long-term pros and cons of continuing their behavior.*

5. <u>**Reactance**</u> – Brehm Theory (1981). When behavioral freedom and autonomy are threatened, the probability and perceived desirability of the Uto-be-lostU behavior will increase.

Both counselors and clients need to understand that reactance is normal. Counselors need to expect and normalize feelings of reactance, especially when clients have been mandated to make a change. Counselors facilitate clients in expressing and clarifying those feelings of reactance. This process allows clients to take back ownership and responsibility for their own choices and decisions related to change.

CURRICULUM:

- ***Session One – Orientation / Pre-Assessment Exercises:*** *The counselor will educate new clients about reactance, and normalize their feelings related to being mandated to change. The counselor will have clients complete the **Freedom Exercise**, and have clients read out loud what they have written.*

- ***Session Two – Feelings Exercise 1:*** *Clients will identify and describe their feelings related to being mandated to change.*

6. <u>**Self-Perception Theory**</u> – D. J. Bem (1972). When people publicly take a position, their commitment to that position increases.
   *It is the client who should present the argument for change.

Counselors need to utilize MI strategies throughout the group process. Counselors will listen, reflect and affirm change talk. The exercises are designed to elicit change talk. Clients reading out loud what they write solidify their own arguments for change.

CURRICULUM:

All exercises are designed to evoke change talk: problem recognition, areas of concern, intentions to change and optimism about the possibility of change. Clients read all completed exercises out loud. This process increases clients' commitments to making change. The counselor also reflects and affirms the clients' commitments. Clients may hear their change talk again by listening to other clients who may give voice to similar reasons for change.

7. <u>**Self-Regulation Theory**</u> – F.H. Kanfer (1986). To trigger change, one would seek to increase the discrepancy between current status and goal. **"Where I see myself going & where I want to be."**

Counselors will utilize the exercises to increase clients' awareness of the discrepancies between current status and goal. The feelings exercises, values clarification and vision exercises, increase clients' awareness of the discrepancies between status and goal and trigger intrinsic desires for change.

CURRICULUM:

- **Session Two-Feelings Exercise 1 & 2:** *Clients are able to clarify feelings related to external mandates to change and feelings related to internal desire for change.*

- **Session Four – Values Exercise 1:** *Clients will identify, prioritize and define their top six values. Clients are then asked to describe how their behavior impacts each of their values and/or which of their values support their behavior. The counselor allows clients to experience the feeling of discomfort related to the discrepancy between their behavior and values.*

- ***Session Five – Vision / Post-Assessment Exercises:*** *Clients present their vision of possible changes and improvements in various areas of their lives that were impacted by their behavior. They will describe their feeling and values related to those changes.*

8. **Value Theory** – M. Rokeach (1979). The Nature of Human Values. Rokeach conceptualized personality as hierarchically organized:

Immediate Behavior & Cognitions
Individual Attitudes
Beliefs
Core Values
Sense of
Personal
Identity

"The further 'in' the shift occurs, the more sweeping will be the resulting change."

CURRICULUM:

- *Session Four – Values Exercise 1:* *Clients will identify, prioritize and define their top six values. Clients are then asked to describe how their behavior impacts each of their values and/or which of their values support their behavior. The counselor allows clients to experience the feeling of discomfort related to the discrepancy between their behavior and values.*

- *Exercise Four – Values Exercise2 (Homework):* *Clients are asked to keep their values in mind for one week and describe the behaviors and/or activities that they engaged in that support each of their values.* ***This exercise allows clients to experience how it feels to decrease the discrepancy between their behavior and values.***

If we understand these conceptual models we have a framework for facilitating motivation and effecting change. William Miller's research showed that a therapist can significantly influence client motivation. "Motivation is not seen as a client trait but the interpersonal process between therapist and client." "How a therapist thinks about motivation and change greatly influences what a therapist does."

I have been inspired and motivated with the results of this process. It returns us to the basics of client centeredness where respect and positive regard of each individual is paramount. MI provides a structure that gives responsibility back to the client for change, relieving counselors of that assumed "burden." Once clients have made a commitment for change, counselors can more successfully provide support and strategies to assist clients in achieving their goals.

Curriculum Outline
For Each Session

OPEN GROUP FORMAT

The Orientation (session one) must be held at a separate time from the motivation group (sessions two-five). All new members must complete the Orientation (session one), before starting the motivation group (sessions two-five). This format allows the motivation group to remain open for new members. Depending on client flow, having an Orientation Session scheduled every week may be necessary.

The client's final session is their presentations of "the vision" they have completed as homework. If clients come for their final session without completing it, they should complete it while the rest of the group is working on a different exercise and present it at the end of group. They will stay after group to complete their post assessment exercises and review them with the facilitator.

SESSION ONE: Orientation
Time Allowed: One hour

Rationale
Based on Daryl Bem's Self-Perception Theory (1972), people learn what they believe in the same way others do, by hearing themselves talk. Facilitating a motivational group allows this process to occur. At orientation, the facilitator starts the process through the use of self-assessment exercises, inherent in the process is the expectation that clients will read what they have written out loud. When people publicly take a position, their commitment to that position increases. It is the clients who should present their arguments for change. Let clients confront their own arguments for change. Allow for discrepancies to build. To confront means to bring together for close examination.

Purpose of this session
The purpose of this session is to prepare the client for the MI group. To do so, the client is informed about group norms, which include: group ethics, self-assessment exercises and the schedule for group attendance. The client is provided an overview of the process they will go through, timeline, material, how materials will be kept from week to week. During this session, the client's baseline level of motivation and confidence will be measured. The client will be oriented to the MI philosophy and become clear about what their next step in treatment will be.

Facilitator Mind Set
Facilitators engage clients by utilizing an empathetic style of reflective listening, accurate understanding, acceptance and respect. Roll with resistance. Trust the process (don't need to push it). The exercises elicit change talk. Listen for and affirm change talk. Let clients hear themselves. Know when to be quiet. Don't debate, argue or confront.

Materials needed for this session
Supplies: folders, pens, clipboards, dry erase board and dry erase pen.

Client Handouts
Group Norms
Facilitator philosophy
Freedom handout
Purpose of the group

Areas of Impact
Stages of Change
Self-Commitment rating
Treatment plan
Group Summary

Other Paperwork
Client sign in sheet
Roster/tracking sheet

Procedures

1. Set up chairs in a circle. Have all chairs the same.

2. Put facilitator name, name of group and the next day and time of group on the board.

3. Have clients sign-in and as the facilitator checks the roster, (Sign-In Handout and Roster are located at the back of this manual, under Forms).

4. Introduce self and the Orientation session by saying, "I will review with you the group norms, expectations and group process. I will also have you complete some self assessment exercises."

5. Have clients briefly introduce themselves: their name, why they are in group, who their counselor is and if they are attending any other groups.

6. Review **Handout 1- Group Norms (p.19)**. The facilitator will review each item on the ethics section, focusing on safety and honesty. Emphasize that honesty plays an important role in this group. Clients will be given an exercise to complete each time they come to group. The more honest clients are in completing their exercises, the more they will gain from the exercises.

7. Distribute a folder to each participant. Have them put their name on it. Explain that you will make copies of the completed exercises at the end of each group, but clients will keep the originals in their folder. The facilitator will offer to keep client's folders week to week or clients can choose to take their folders with them, as long as them bring them to group each week.

8. Continue on with the handout, emphasizing attendance policy. Clients will be allowed only one excused absence, if they call in advance. Emphasize the importance of attending each group, over the next four weeks, so they can benefit from the accumulative effect of the exercises.

9. The facilitator will explain the group process. Even though clients will be in a group setting, they will be doing their own individual work. No cross talk or debating what people say or write is allowed. This provides safety, so clients can speak freely and write what is on their mind. Everyone will complete the exercise and then read it out loud. Spelling and grammar don't matter. They will benefit from hearing themselves read out-loud, what they have written. Explain, that at times, is it is like a one room schoolhouse, where people will be working on different exercises during the same group session.

   Highlight the basic process for each week:
   a. Sign in
   b. Check in (5 minutes total)
   c. Reflect on Change (Quote)
   d. Homework Review
   e. Explain the group exercise.
   f. Participants do the exercise.
   g. Participants will read their exercises out loud
   h. Participants will fill out the group summary, while facilitator makes copies of the exercises.
   i. Hand back originals for clients to put into their folders. Collect group summaries. Collect folders.

10. Review **Handout 2 – Philosophy (p.20).** The facilitator talks about self and philosophy of working with people. Emphasize experience in various settings. Labeling does not work. Express desire to get to know who each of them is.

11. The facilitator discusses feelings related to being mandated or leveraged to change. Brehm's (1981) Reactance Theory states, that perceived threats to personal freedom and choice will elicit behaviors designed to demonstrate and restore that freedom. When behavioral freedom and autonomy are threatened, the probability and perceived desirability of the to-be-lost behavior will increase. It is normal to feel resistant when independence

and freedom of choice have been taken away. Recognize that most people make changes on their own. The purpose of this group process is to decide what each of them wants to do, even if a System (i.e. Legal, Child Welfare, Medical, and Mental Health) is mandating them to make changes. Whether or not they want to change is their choice.

12. Review **Handout 3 – Freedom Exercise (p.22)**. Spend the next few minutes answering the four questions. (5 minutes) Individual clients will read all their answers on the page, before going to the next person. For each person, on question four, where they rate their level of freedom, whatever number they circled, ask why it is not lower on the scale. Also ask what they would have to do to make it higher on the scale.

13. Distribute **Handout 4 – Purpose of Group (p.23).** Read it out loud to group. Ask them what they related to. If people are not focused on what they want to do, it will help them focus. If they have a focus, it will help them clarify it. Explain that getting involved with a System (i.e. Legal, Child Welfare, Medical, and Mental Health) may cause people to lose a sense of themselves, and they may end up doing whatever they think will get them through. This group gives them the opportunity to focus on themselves and what if anything they want to do, regarding changing their behavior.

14. Distribute **Handout 5 – Areas of Impact (p. 25)**. Have them complete Part A first. When everyone is done, explain Part B. This is introduced with the phrase "Select from the list above the items you have circled 3 or 4. List those areas in order of importance." When everyone is finished, have them each read Part B (their prioritized list) out loud.

    Facilitator Hint: If they say they don't have any 3's or 4's, have them prioritize their twos. If they have all ones, don't worry about it (roll with resistance).

15. Review and discuss **Handout Wheel of Change (p.27).** This exercise is based on Prochaska and DiClemente's process of change, which defines several stages that people normally pass through in the process of changing their behavior. The facilitator explains, "I want you to understand how people change. It has been studied a lot, and recently studied how people struggling with addictions change. The researchers realized people change in similar ways, they go through stages".

Draw the wheel and write the stages of change on the board.

Educate clients on the wheel of change by describing each stage. Use an example that is not a hot topic.

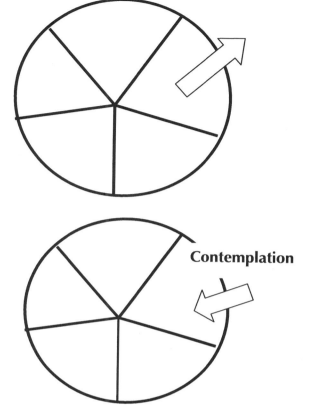

Precontemplation

Example:

I have a car that keeps breaking down. My friends are giving me rides. My friends say, 'You need to get a new car'. I say, 'No I don't.'

This is Precontemplation. "I am hearing some concerns regarding my car, but I don't think I have a problem." This is an indication that this person has not entered the wheel.

Example:

Let's say my friends quit giving me rides. As a result I am late to work. My boss is upset with me. My kids aren't getting to their activities. And it is causing a safety issue, late on the road at night. I'm becoming aware of risks.

Contemplation

Once awareness of risks begins, people enter the wheel. The first stage is Contemplation. In this stage people consider the possibility of change and at the same time, reject it. The primary feeling is ambivalence. In conflict situations, ambivalence is normal and is a critical obstacle to change. A person feels two ways about change. On one hand they think about the need for change. On the other hand, they reject it.

Example of ambivalence:

If my friends tell me the reasons I should get a new car, I will tell them all the reasons why I can't get a new car. And if they tell me why I shouldn't get another car, I will tell them all the reasons I should.

For a more serious problem, this is a painful place to be stuck.
(Ex. "These are the reasons I need to leave this relationship, and these are the reasons I don't").

People can become immobilized when feelings of ambivalence are left unresolved. Also in past treatment experiences, counselors or other people in authority may not have been aware of ambivalence as a normal stage of change and may have labeled clients as resistant.

Becoming aware of risks is not enough for change to occur. This is based on Ronald Rogers' Protection Motivation Theory, a health beliefs model. Motivation for change depends on the presence of a sufficient degree of perceived risk, in combination with sufficient self-efficacy. You need two things for change, awareness of risks and self-efficacy, the belief that change is possible.

Returning to my example of getting a new car:

Example: *I don't know what to look for under the hood of a car, to make sure I'm getting a good one. I don't know how to talk to a car salesman, or go to the bank for a loan.*

If one doesn't know how to do these things, their self- efficacy is low. This means their belief that change is possible is low.

Example: *Now, let's say I tell a friend and my friend says, I know someone who is great with cars, give him a call. I make an appointment and I feel a little bit of hope.*

When this occurs, they move into Preparation stage – They are leaning toward the possibility of change. This stage provides a small window of opportunity. It can close as quickly as it opens.

Example: *Let's say my friend's friend doesn't show for the appointment to meet with me. How do I feel? Where might I go in the wheel? On the other hand, let's say he does show up and takes me to ten car lots and tells me what to look for under the hood of a car, and how to talk to a salesman and talk to a loan officer at a bank. Now I begin to feel hopeful and I think I can make the change with some additional help.*

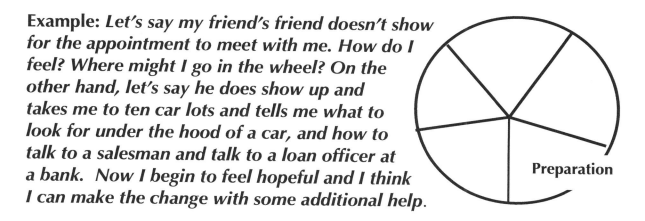

Preparation

As one's self-efficacy increases, they move from Preparation into Action. Most treatment agencies are *action* models. That means the minute a client walks through the door they expect them to be at the action stage.
But what if they are in *Pre-contemplation or Contemplation?* If they come to treatment in Pre-contemplation and/or Contemplation, they need to learn about risks and resolve their ambivalence. In Action they have made up their mind to change. They want to make a change. If they are in Action, treatment will teach them the strategies to make the change.

(Ex. I've already made my mind up to get a car; just teach me what I need to know to accomplish my goal).

Once clients have made changes in their behavior, they enter Maintenance. In the A&D treatment community, clients are considered in maintenance when they have abstained for 6-12 months. While in this stage, clients have achieved their initial goal and are working on other issues that were impacted by their behavior to help maintain their goal and keep their life moving forward.

Returning to my example:

Once I bought the car, I began to take care of other areas of my life. (i.e. making up time at work, and getting my kids back into their activities).

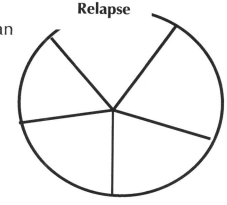

Most people don't change from point A to point B in a linear fashion. Change is a process. It is more like an upward spiral than a line. For example, most people who quit smoking try many times, before they finally quit. Each time leads them closer to their goal. In the next stage, notice that Relapse is in the wheel, as a normal part of the change process.

In the treatment community, relapse sometimes isn't handled well. It is not uncommon for clients to be sent to jail or kicked out of treatment, due to a relapse. After a relapse, people often experience a sense of hopelessness and despair and may give up on their goal. These internal attributions can be altered, by educating clients about relapse.

Counselors can say:

Relapse is normal. It is about returning to old patterns and behaviors in vulnerable times and situations. At those times and in those situations you weren't prepared to handle them differently. If you acknowledge your relapse and stay in the wheel, and keep your goal in mind, you can move through the stages. In Action, you can learn strategies to strengthen those vulnerable areas and situations to prevent relapse from happening again. You need strategies to learn how to handle things differently.

16. **Handout 6- Wheel of Change (p.27)** Ask everyone to shade in where they think they are on the wheel as of today. One can be a sliver of one stage and much of another. Acknowledge that change is a process. Where ever one is, is ok. Ask everyone to read or show where they are on the wheel.

17. **Handout 7 Commitment Rating** & **Confidence Rating (p.29)**. Have them rate their commitment level to accomplishing their goal, however they define it. Also have them rate their confidence level, how confident they feel that they have the skills to accomplish their goal. Group members read both ratings out loud.

18. Have clients hand in 4 exercises, (Handouts 3, 5, 6, & 7) making sure their names and the date is on them.

19. Have them read and sign the **Treatment Plans – Handout 8 (pg. 31),** that the facilitator prepared while they were doing the exercises. In addition, have them complete the **Handout - Group Summary (p.32).** Ask clients not to leave as you go make copies of their exercises.

20. Return their original exercises back to clients to put in their folders. Collect from clients their Group Summaries and Treatment Plans.

21. Remind them of the meeting time next week. Thank them for their work.

Group Norms

Group Ethics
Safety
Respect
Confidentiality
Honesty

Group Materials
Folder
Exercises

Group Time
1 x a week, for 4 weeks

Missed Appointments
Allowable, one—with advanced notice.

Where do I go after completing motivation group?

Group Process
Be in group on time.
Fill out Sign-in form
Identify clients who completed vision homework
Identify clients who will be receiving vision homework
Spend 5 minutes with group for check-in process
Review quote
Review completed homework
Counselor explains exercises
Clients do identified exercise
Clients present their exercises in group
Review homework
5 minute check-out process

Counselor's Philosophy

Labels:

I'm not going to label you (e.g. a criminal, or an addict) or force you to accept a label because research does not support that as a way people change. Most people are concerned about being stigmatized and being labeled, because that is not ***who you are***. Just like if I had cancer; I would not like to be labeled the "cancer patient". If I had cancer, it may be something that affects different areas of my life, but it is not, ***who I am.*** My name is Ann Fields… that is who I am…and In this group I want to get to know who you are.

Mandated to Change:

All of you have been mandated or leveraged to change due to concerns regarding your behavior, past and/or present. Some of these concerns may not necessarily be your own.

When you are mandated or leveraged to change, your life may feel like it is not your own. It may feel confusing and frustrating; like your world has been turned upside down. Your choices and decisions don't feel like your own. Reactance is normal. In this group we will discuss your feelings related to being mandated or leveraged to change and explore what, if anything, you may want to do about making changes in your lives.

Name: *John* .   Date: _____

FREEDOM

1. Describe your loss of freedom of choice and independence, once you entered the system, (i.e. Legal, DHS, Mental Health, and Medical).

Even though my freedom had been taken, I still acted as if I was free creating a much bigger problem.

2. What do you hope for and expect, regarding your freedom of choice and independence once you are no longer involved in the system?

True freedom/full freedom

3. What disappoints you now, regarding your freedom of choice and independence?

I'm still not free.

4. On a 1-10 scale, with 1 being no freedom and 10 being completely free, rate your sense of freedom of choice and independence as of today?

No freedom   Totally free

0-------1-------2-------3-------④-------5-------6-------7-------8-------9-------10

Name: _____   Date: _____

FREEDOM

1. Describe your loss of freedom of choice and independence, once you entered the system, (i.e. Legal, DHS, Mental Health, and Medical).

2. What do you hope for and expect, regarding your freedom of choice and independence once you are no longer involved in the system?

3. What disappoints you now, regarding your freedom of choice and independence?

4. On a 1-10 scale, with 1 being no freedom and 10 being completely free, rate your sense of freedom of choice and independence as of today?

No freedom   Totally free

0-------1-------2-------3-------4-------5-------6-------7-------8-------9-------10

Purpose of Group

This group is to help you gain back some control over your own choices and decisions about this time in your life, by giving you a chance to reevaluate your life, and what you may want to do about the concerns related to your behavior (i.e. anger, substance use, taking your medications, etc.). What you do with this information is up to you. The final choice and decisions about any changes you make in your lives is always your own.

Re Evaluation Process—When feelings of confusion, anger and fear appear, in response to the need for a change in your life; compounded with feelings of not knowing who you are anymore and the direction your life is going, it is difficult to know where to begin. Not knowing where to begin is very common and some of the universal questions people start asking are:

Who Am I?
Where Am I Going?
What Is My Purpose?
How Do I Get There?

The first step to help you find some answers to these questions is to go through this group.

Pre-Assessment Exercise

Name: _John_   Date:_____

Areas of Impact Assessment **(Part A)**

On a scale of 1-4, with 1 being the *least* impacted, and 4 being the *most,* please circle the level of negative impact your behavior has had on the different areas of your life.

Relationships	1	2	③	4
Work	1	②	3	4
Financial	1	②	3	4
Legal	1	②	3	4
Family	①	2	3	4
Education	1	②	3	4
Community	1	②	3	4
Physical Health	1	②	3	4
Emotional Health	1	2	③	4
Spirituality	①	2	3	4
Hobbies/Interests	1	2	③	4
Social Life	1	2	③	4
Character/Morals/Values	1	2	③	4
Self-esteem	1	②	3	4

(Part B) List the areas most impacted (3 or 4) by your behavior, in order of importance.

1. *relationships*

2. *character, morals, values*

3. *emotional health*

4. *hobbies, interests*

5. *social life*

6.

7.

Pre Assessment Exercise

Name: _____   Date:_____

Areas of Impact Assessment **(Part A)**
On a scale of 1-4, with 1 being the *least* impacted, and 4 being the *most,* please circle the level of negative impact your behavior has had on the different areas of your life.

Relationships	1	2	3	4
Work	1	2	3	4
Financial	1	2	3	4
Legal	1	2	3	4
Family	1	2	3	4
Education	1	2	3	4
Community	1	2	3	4
Physical Health	1	2	3	4
Emotional Health	1	2	3	4
Spirituality	1	2	3	4
Hobbies/Interests	1	2	3	4
Social Life	1	2	3	4
Character/Morals/Values	1	2	3	4
Self-esteem	1	2	3	4

(Part B) List the areas most impacted (3 or 4) by your behavior, in order of importance.

1.

2.

3.

4.

5.

6.

7.

8.

Pre-Assessment Exercise

Name: _John_   Date: _____

PROCHASKA-DICLEMENTE'S WHEEL OF CHANGE

Please read the definition of each stage of change, written below, and shade in the area of the wheel that identifies where you are, in the process of changing your behavior.

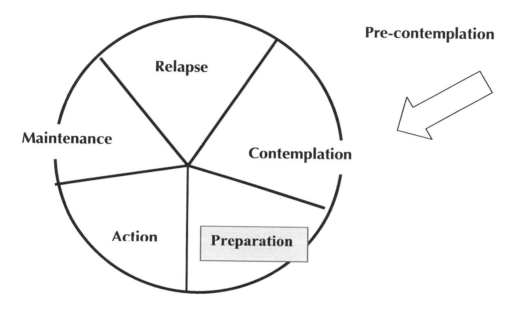

The Six Stages Of Change:

1. Pre-contemplation-**You do not think that your behavior is a problem.**

2. Contemplation-**You are considering the possibility of changing your behavior and at the same time rejecting the idea of change.**

3. Preparation-**You are leaning toward change, seriously considering no longer engaging in your behavior.**

4. Action-**You are taking steps to no longer engage in your behavior.**

5. Maintenance-**You are identifying and using strategies to prevent relapse and addressing other areas of your life.**

6. Relapse-**You are renewing the processes of contemplation, preparation and action and not giving up on your goal.**

Pre-Assessment Exercise

Name:_____   Date: _____

PROCHASKA-DICLEMENTE'S WHEEL OF CHANGE

Please read the definition of each stage of change, written below, and shade in the area of the wheel that identifies where you are, in the process of changing your behavior.

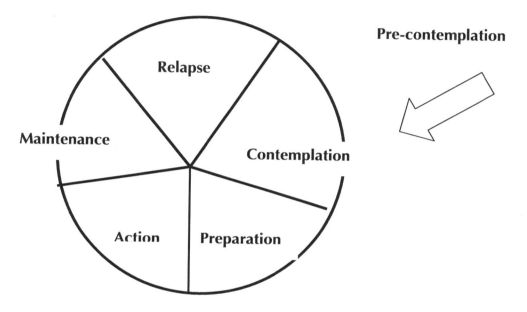

The Six Stages Of Change:

1. Pre-contemplation-**You do not think that your behavior is a problem.**

2. Contemplation-**You are considering the possibility of changing your behavior and at the same time rejecting the idea of change.**

3. Preparation-**You are leaning toward change, seriously considering no longer engaging in your behavior.**

4. Action-**You are taking steps to no longer engage in your behavior.**

5. Maintenance-**You are identifying and using strategies to prevent relapse and addressing other areas of your life.**

6. Relapse-**You are renewing the processes of contemplation, preparation and action and not giving up on your goal.**

Pre-Assessment Exercise

Name: _John_

Date: _____

Self-Commitment Rating

At this moment, how important is it to you to change your behavior? How hard are you willing to work and how much are you willing to do? Answer this question by writing a number from 0-100 in the designated space below, using the following scale as a guide.

1	25	50	75	100
Not important at all	Less important than most other things I would like to achieve	About as important as most of the other things I would like to achieve	More important than most of the other things I would like to achieve	The most important thing in my life

Write your goal importance rating (from 0-100) here: __65%__

Self-Confidence Rating (Do I believe I can succeed?)

How confident are you that you could make a change if you wanted to? Answer this question by writing a number from 0-100 in the designated space below, using the following scale as a guide.

0%	50%	100%
Not at all confident that I will achieve my goal	50-50 chance I will achieve my goal	Totally Confident I will Achieve my goal.

Write your confidence rating (from 0% - 100%) here: __100%__

Pre-Assessment Exercise

Name: _____   Date: _____

Self-Commitment Rating

At this moment, how important is it to you to change your behavior? How hard are you willing to work and how much are you willing to do? Answer this question by writing a number from 0-100 in the designated space below, using the following scale as a guide.

1	25	50	75	100
Not important at all	Less important than most other things I would like to achieve	About as important as most of the other things I would like to achieve	More important than most of the other things I would like to achieve	The most important thing in my life

Write your goal importance rating (from 0-100) here: _____

Self-Confidence Rating (Do I believe I can succeed?)

How confident are you that you could make a change if you wanted to? Answer this question by writing a number from 0-100 in the designated space below, using the following scale as a guide.

0%	50%	100%
Not at all confident that I will achieve my goal	50-50 chance I will achieve my goal	Totally Confident I will Achieve my goal.

Write your confidence rating (from 0% - 100%) here: _____

Treatment Plan

Name: _John_   Date: _6/02/03_

GROUP: MOTIVATION GROUP
GOAL: To increase awareness of risks, level of self-efficacy and intrinsic desire for change.

Objective	Activity	Responsible Party	Frequency	Date Completed
A. Taking steps to reduce and/or no longer engage in your behavior.	1. Self-reports last time engaged in behavior.	Client	1x/wk	
B. To assess stage of change, impact of behavior and level of commitment and confidence to making changes in your behavior.	2. Attend orientation prior to entering motivation group. Complete all pre-assessment exercises.	Client	1x	**6/2/03**
C. To increase awareness of risks of behavior and level of self-efficacy to change.	3. Attend all four motivation group sessions. Complete all group exercises and homework assignments.	Client	4x	
D. To reassess stages of change and commitment and confidence levels to making changes in your behavior and create a vision of the hoped for changes and improvements in the different areas of your life.	4. Complete post-assessment exercises and present vision	Client	1x	
E. To collaborate and plan your next steps.	5. Contact referral counselor / provider after completing group.	Client	1x	

John
Client signature

6/2/03
Date

Counselor signature

6/2/03
Date

Treatment Plan

Name:_____   Date:_____

GROUP: MOTIVATION GROUP

GOAL: To increase awareness of risks, level of self-efficacy and intrinsic desire for change.

Objective	Activity	Responsible Party	Frequency	Date Completed
A. Taking steps to reduce and/or no longer engage in your behavior.	1. Self-reports last time engaged in behavior.	Client	1 x wk	
B. To assess stage of change, impact of behavior and level of commitment and confidence to making changes in your behavior.	2. Attend orientation prior to entering motivation group. Complete all pre-assessment exercises.	Client	1 x	
C. To increase awareness of risks of behavior and level of self-efficacy to change.	3. Attend all four motivation group sessions. Complete all group exercises and homework assignments.	Client	4 x	
D. To reassess stages of change and commitment and confidence levels to making changes in your behavior and create a vision of the hoped for changes and improvements in the different areas of your life.	4. Complete post-assessment exercises and present vision.	Client	1 x	
E. To collaborate and plan next steps.	5. Contact referral counselor / provider after completing group.	Client	1 x	

_____
Client signature

_____
Counselor signature

_____
Date

_____
Date

Group Summary (Client Weekly Update)

GROUP: Motivation Group

Facilitator: _____   Date: 6/02/03 _____

Client's Name: *John* _____   Group Time: 90 minutes _____

Right now I'm feeling: *Nervous*

The topic of group today was: *Orientation, stages of change*

What I learned about myself in this session: *That it is normal to feel two ways about change.*

How I'm feeling about group now: *Looking forward to learning more.*

_____

Counselor Notes:

Facilitator Signature: _____ Date: _____

SESSION TWO: Feelings
Time Allowed: 90 minutes

Rationale for this session
This session is designed to provide the opportunity to normalize reactance Brehm's Theory (1981) states that when behavioral freedom and autonomy are threatened, the probability and perceived desirability of the to-be-lost behavior will increase.

Purpose
This session helps move clients away from external mandates toward intrinsic desires for change. They need to vent their feelings about being mandated (whatever form the mandate takes). Also they may acknowledge feelings e.g. relief or worry, that suggest intrinsic awareness of their need for change. The process allows clients to begin to clarify need for change and articulate the feelings related to change.

The second exercise provides the opportunity to clarify feelings related to the areas of their lives they identified as impacted by their behavior in Session One. This adds another layer to the awareness for change and begins to evoke change talk.

Facilitator Mind Set
The facilitator engages clients by utilizing an empathetic style of reflective listening, accurate understanding, acceptance and respect. Roll with resistance. Trust the process (one doesn't need to push it). The exercises elicits change talk. Listen for and affirm change talk. Let clients hear themselves. Know when to be quiet. Don't debate, argue or confront. Remember reactance is normal. Clients need to present their own arguments for change.

Materials needed for this session
Supplies: folders, pens, clipboards, dry erase board and dry erase pen.

Client Handouts:
> **Feelings Exercise 1& 2.** For **Exercise 2**, clients will need **Handout # 5– Areas of Impact**; the self-assessment that they completed in the Orientation session, located in their folder.
> Group Summary

Other Paperwork:

Client Sign In sheet

Roster/tracking sheet

Vision homework: for clients completing their third group session.

Post Assessment Handouts 16-18 and **Client Satisfaction Survey Handout 19**, for clients presenting their <u>Vision</u> in this group.

Handouts 21 (Quotes) & **22** (Poem), for clients who have completed the Motivation Group.

Procedures

1. Clients sign in and the facilitator checks the roster. (Sign in sheet and Rosters, **pg. 94-95).**

2. The process for the check in is as follows: Name. Date of last time they engaged in their behavior. Why they are in the group. Identify other groups they may be attending and the counselors they see. Identify how they are feeling and how they are taking care of themselves. Check in with them to verify if they have done their homework. Notify those who are going to receive their vision homework to stay after group. Check in with the members who are completing the group to see if they have done their Vision Homework..

If they have not completed their Vision homework, they will do the Vision exercise **(Handout 20, pg.97-98)** in the final group session as part of their exercise. They will stay after group to complete the **Post-Assessment** exercises and compare their Pre and Post Assessment exercises with the facilitator. (Their **Pre Assessment exercises Handouts 5- 7**, are in their folders). Once they have completed the entire group, the facilitator will disperse **Handouts 21-** Quotes and **22 - Poem, (pg. 85-86)**. These two handouts are given as a form of closure and to say good-bye to each client.

3. Put the quote on the board. Ask them to reflect on the quote that is about change. Ask how they relate to the quote in terms of changes they have made in their life, now or in their past.

4. Review homework.

5. Distribute the **Post Assessment** exercises and **Client Satisfaction Survey** to those presenting their vision and completing the group. The **Post**

Assessment exercises are **Handouts 16-18** and **Client Satisfaction Survey, Handout 19**. All the handouts are to be completed in the group session.

6. Distribute the make-up exercise to the clients who have already completed this group exercise in a prior group session.

7. Distribute for this session, **Handout 9 – Feelings Exercise 1 & 2 (p.39 and p.40).** Instruct them to do the Feelings Exercise 1. The facilitator will read the directions on the handout to the group. As the clients are working on first exercise, the facilitator will explain the directions for the make-up exercises to the other clients.

8. Facilitating **Feelings Exercise 2**. The facilitator will have the clients retrieve the "Areas of Impact" exercise, they completed at Orientation **(Handout 5)** from their folder. The next step is to have them focus on (Part B) where they have prioritized and listed the areas of their lives impacted by their behavior. The task is to have them identify feelings related to each of the identified areas. Discussion of feelings will follow once all clients have completed the exercise.

9. The Group Process: The facilitator will have each member read out loud both the feeling words they circled and their paragraph from **Feelings Exercise 1.**

10. In the **Feelings Exercise 2**, the facilitator will explain to the clients that this exercise may bring up vulnerable feelings. It is important for everyone to trust the process and to let them hear themselves say out loud what they have written. Allow them time to describe their feelings related to the areas of their lives impacted by their behavior. If clients can only articulate a simple association (ex. Family: angry) that is "OK". Thank each person as they finish and move to the next individual. Once all the clients have had the opportunity to express themselves, let the session end. This allows them to experience the process. (Don't add something to fill time).

11. Have the clients doing make-up exercise present their work in the group session.

12. Have the members who are completing their final session, present their vision. Have them read their summary page and then their vision.

13. Have all the clients turn in their exercises. The clients will fill out the **Group Summary Sheet (pg.96)** while the facilitator makes copies of their exercises. The facilitator will return the original exercises back to the clients. Have the members put the originals back into the folders. The facilitator will collect the group summaries and folders as they leave.

14. The facilitator reviews the **Pre and Post Assessment** exercises with those clients who are completing their final session. The Pre-assessment exercises are in their folders. When a client completes their final session, they will receive their folder and a copy of the **Quotes (Handout 21)** and the **Poem (Handout 22).**

15. The clients that need to complete the Vision Homework **(Handout 20, pg. 97-98)** will remain after the group session to review the exercise with the facilitator. The clients will take out three exercises they have completed from their folder: **Areas of Impact** – (Part B), **Feelings** underlined, and the six **Values** they prioritized. From the exercises, the clients will complete the vision exercise summary sheet, **(pg 97).** The facilitator will review the direction under **Part B** of the Vision exercise for clients to complete at home.

Name: *John*   Date: _____

Exercise 1. Review the list of feelings below and underline all the feelings you remember having on the day you were mandated or leveraged to change your behavior. After underlining your feelings, please write a short paragraph, on the following page, describing those feelings.

Exercise 2. Take the orientation exercise, **Areas of Impact,** out of your folder. Review the list of feelings below and write the feelings you are currently having next to each of the areas of your life that you prioritized on (Part B).

FEELINGS

Vulnerable	*Mad*	*Worried*	Confused
Loss of Control	Sad	*Powerlessness*	
Empty	Fearful	Frustrated	Rage
Startled	Disappointed	*Happy*	Hopeless
Numb	Irritated	Shocked	Angry Jealous
Restless	Content	Belittled	Oppressed
Inadequate	Stunned	Tired	Jumpy *Guilty*
Outraged	Depressed	*Satisfied*	Invisible
Exhausted	Remorseful	Glad	*Embarrassed*
Relaxed	*Anxious*	*Relief*	*Nervous*

Name: _John_   Date: _____

FEELINGS

Vulnerable- after not complying with treatment the first time, I was given no choice but to engage in a group.

Worried-Had many concerns that this wouldn't be a program I could see myself completing.

Mad- That once again that I was finding myself back starting all over again.

Happy-That there was someone willing to work with me.

Powerlessness-Knew my options were completely worn out.

Guilty-Because I didn't give myself a real chance the first time.

Satisfied-Felt it was really a possibility.

Embarrassed-Because I have been still dealing with the same charge since 1998 and still haven't taken care of it.

Relaxed- Felt completely satisfied that my concerns were met.
Anxious- Eager to get started.

Relief- Because I truly felt like I could change.

Nervous- Because I know I am just one step away from everything I just left.

Name: _____   Date: _____

Exercise 1. Review the list of feelings below and underline all the feelings you remember having on the day you were mandated or leveraged to change your behavior. After underlining your feelings, please write a short paragraph, on the following page, describing those feelings.

Exercise 2. Take the orientation exercise, **Areas of Impact,** out of your folder. Review the list of feelings below and write the feelings you are currently having next to each of the areas of your life that you prioritized on (Part B).

FEELINGS

Vulnerable	Mad	Worried	Confused
Loss of Control	Sad	Powerlessness	
Empty	Fearful	Frustrated	Rage
Startled	Disappointed	Happy	Hopeless
Numb	Irritated	Shocked	Angry Jealous
Restless	Content	Belittled	Oppressed
Inadequate	Stunned	Tired	Jumpy Guilty
Outraged	Depressed	Satisfied	Invisible
Exhausted	Remorseful	Glad	Embarrassed
Relaxed	Anxious	Relief	Nervous

Name: _____   Date: _____

FEELINGS

Exercise 2

Name: _John_ _____ Date: _____

Areas of Impact Assessment (Part A)

On a scale of 1-4, with 1 being the *least* impacted, and 4 being the *most,* please circle the level of negative impact your behavior has had on the different areas of your life.

Relationships	1	2	③	4
Work	1	②	3	4
Financial	1	②	3	4
Legal	1	②	3	4
Family	①	2	3	4
Education	1	②	3	4
Community	1	②	3	4
Physical Health	1	②	3	4
Emotional Health	1	2	③	4
Spirituality	①	2	3	4
Hobbies/Interests	1	2	③	4
Social Life	1	2	③	4
Character/Morals/Values	1	2	③	4
Self-esteem	1	②	3	4

(Part B) List the areas most impacted (3 or 4) by your behavior, in order of importance.

1. *relationships—worried and disappointed*

2. *character, morals, values—empty*

3. *emotional health—sad, frustrated*

4. *hobbies, interests—worried and anxious*

5. *social life—nervous, confused, lonely*

6.

7.

SESSION THREE: Pro's and Cons

Time Allowed: 90 minutes

Rationale

Janis and Mann's decisional balance theory (1977) states that decision -making is a process of weighing cognitively the pros and cons of change.

Purpose of this Session

This session focuses on client's ambivalence, the "good things" and "not so good things" about their behavior. It serves to develop an awareness of risks by weighing the costs and benefits of one's behavior. It also focuses on the client's ability to assess their degree of self-efficacy to change. Emphasis is placed on the power of the short term "pros" and options to successfully alter or avoid engaging in the behavior.

Facilitator Mind Set

Let the client do the identification. Listen for their identification of problems associated with their behavior (problem recognition). Affirm areas where the client is demonstrating strength in identifying options to avoid or alter behavior. Affirm the client's recognition of additional areas of concern. The facilitator also provides a menu of options to assist clients in making additional choices. Allowing them to take ownership of their strengths to address areas of concern builds intrinsic motivation.

Materials needed for this session

Supplies: folders, pens, clipboards, dry erase board and dry erase pen.

Client Handouts

Individual exercise: Handouts - **10a & 10b,** for clients who missed the group Brainstorming.
Short Term Pros
Altered States Descriptor
Homework: Menu of Alternatives & Altered States Categorizer

Other Paperwork

Client Sign In sheet
Roster/tracking sheet
Vision homework – if the client will be completing his/her third group session.
Post Assessment Handouts – 16-18 and **Handout 19- Client Satisfaction Survey** for the clients presenting their Vision in this group.
Handouts 21 (Quotes) & **22** (Poem) are for clients who have completed the Motivation Group.

© **Hollifield Associates / 2004**

Procedures

1. Clients sign in and the facilitator checks the roster. (Sign in sheet and Rosters, **pg. 94-95).**

2. The process for the check in is as follows: Name. Date of last time they engaged in their behavior. Why they are in the group. Identify other groups they may be attending and the counselors they see. Identify how they are feeling and how they are taking care of themselves. Check in with them to verify if they have done their homework. Notify those who are going to receive their vision homework to stay after group. Check in with the members who are completing the group to see if they have done their Vision Homework.

   If they have not completed their Vision homework, they will do the Vision exercise **(Handout 20, pg. 97-98)** in the final group session as part of their exercise. They will stay after group to complete the **Post-Assessment** exercises and compare their Pre and Post Assessment exercises with the facilitator. (Their **Pre Assessment exercises Handouts 5-7**, are in their folders). Once they have completed the entire group, the facilitator will disperse **Handouts 21-** Quotes and **22** - Poem, (**pg. 85-86**). These two handouts are given as a form of closure and to say good-bye to each client.

3. Put the quote on the board. Ask them to reflect on the quote that is about change. Ask how they relate to the quote in terms of changes they have made in their life, now or in their past.

4. Review homework.

5. Distribute the **Post Assessment** exercises and **Client Satisfaction Survey** to those presenting their vision and completing the group. The **Post Assessment** exercises are **Handouts 16-18** and **Survey, Handout19-Client Satisfaction**. All the handouts are to be completed in the group session.

6. Distribute the make-up exercise to clients who have already completed this group exercise in a prior group session.

7. Brainstorming Exercise - *Draw Short Term and Long Term Pros and Cons grid on the board.* **Tell group that this is probably an exercise they've done before, when trying to make an important decision in their lives. It's about weighing out the pros and cons, prior to making a decision.** *"Today we are going to look at the short and long term pros and cons of your behavior. This exercise is not meant to trigger you, but we will start the exercise by looking at the short-term pros of your behavior. "What are some of the good things about engaging in your behavior?" What does it do for you?' "What are you hoping for or expecting by engaging in your behavior?"* **Brainstorm with the group and write their responses down.**

   After filling up the short term pro grid switch to the long-term pro box and ask them, *"When you engage in your behavior today, what are you hoping will happen as a result of your behavior, a year from now?"* **Clients will not be able to come up with**

too many answers. Place a zero in the long-term pro grid. After looking at both sides of the short and long-term pro grid, state to the group, "I call this the <u>power of the short-term pros.</u> **(Highlight the short-term pro box)** "Engaging in your behavior is about immediate gratification."

Shift to the short-term cons grid and ask them, "What are some not so good things that can happen in an hour, a day or week as a result of engaging in your behavior." **After filling up the grid explain how the short-term pros and short-term cons are connected.** "When we feel bad we usually want to feel better, so this con box can also trigger our desire to re-engage in our behavior." **Emphasize that this is another example of how powerful the short-term pro box is.**

Next shift to the long-term cons grid and ask the group, "If we don't change and continue to engage in our behavior, what can get worse 1-2 years from now?" **Fill up the long-term cons grid with the group's responses.**

Now tell the group, "When people change their behavior, the short-term consequences start to go away, and that feels good." **Draw an x through the short-term cons box.** "Now they think their work is done, but what did they forget about?" **Re-emphasize the power of the short-term pros box.** "These short-term pros can trigger lapses, so it is important to find other ways to take care of these short-term pros." **This leads to the next exercise.**

*(If a client misses this session and has to make it up, give them a blank pros and cons grid **(Handout 10a, p.47.** Also give them a copy of the brainstorm grid **Handout 10b, p.48)** to assist them in completing their grid).

8.   **Handout 10 - Short term Pros Exercise (p.50).** Have the clients identify what their individual short-term pros are and answer questions 1-3. When clients complete the exercise have them read it out loud.

9.   Have some of clients take turns reading parts of **Handout 11- Alternative States Descriptor, (p.51).** Ask the clients what they thought it meant. Emphasize that when they are thinking of their own alternatives to their behavior, to consider their body chemistry.

10. <u>Assign Homework</u> : **Handout 12– Menu of Alternatives, (pg. 55-56).** Take the list of alternatives and ask them to mark the ones that they would be willing to do. With the items they have marked, have them use **the Altered State Categorizer, (pg. 57)** to list the activities they selected, next to each of the following categories: physical, relaxation, cognitive, creative, meditation. On the bottom half of the handout ask them to list those activities they would be willing to engage in to help alter / avoid their behavior.

11. Remind them the homework will be reviewed the next week (bring it back).

12. Have the clients doing make-up exercises present their work in the group session.

13. Have the members who are completing their final session, present their vision. Have them read their summary page and then their vision.

14. Have all the clients turn in their exercises. The clients will fill out the **Group Summary** sheet (pg.96), while the facilitator makes copies of their exercises. The facilitator will return the original exercises back to the clients. Have the members put the originals back into the folders. The facilitator will collect the group summaries and folders as they leave.

15. The facilitator reviews the **Pre and Post Assessment** exercises with those clients who are completing their final session. The Pre-assessment exercises are in their folders. When a client completes their final session, they will receive their folder and a copy of the **Quotes (Handout 21)** and the **Poem (Handout 22).**

16. The clients that need to complete the Vision Homework **(Handout 20 pg. 97-98)** will remain after the group session to review the exercise with the facilitator. The clients will take out three exercises they have completed from their folder: **Areas of Impact –** (Part B), **Feelings** underlined, and the six **Values** they prioritized. From the exercises, the clients will complete the vision exercise summary sheet, **(pg 97).** The facilitator will review the direction under **Part B** of the Vision exercise for clients to complete at home.

17. Facilitator copies brainstorming chart from the board, types it out for next session.

Name: *John*   Date: _____

Write the short and long term pros and cons of your behavior.

SHORT TERM	LONG TERM
PROS *Energy* *Stress* *Focus* *Social* *Acceptance*	**PROS** *None*
CONS *Financial* *Legal* *Jail* *No driving* *Worry* *Stress* *Probation* *Labeling* *Treatment* *No freedom*	**CONS** *Financial* *Jail / prison* *Emotional health* *Physical health* *Family* *Employment* *Relationship* *Self-esteem* *Death*

Name: _____   Date: _____

Write the short and long term pros and cons of your behavior.

SHORT TERM	LONG TERM
PROS	PROS
CONS	CONS

Group Brainstorm

Write the short and long term pros and cons of your behavior.

SHORT TERM

LONG TERM

PROS Multi-tasked Enjoyment Filled a void "Cool" Forget about things Blocks out the world Increase money Increase sex Image Relax Heighten Emotions Dulls Emotions Stress Energy Appetite Social/acceptance Focus Trance	**PROS** None

CONS
LOSSES:
    Money
    Energy
    Health-physical, mental
    Employment
    Relationships
    Family
    Freedom
    Reliability
    Dependability
    Trust
    Credibility
INCREASES:
    Anxiety
    Procrastination
    Depression
    Treatment
    Hermit Lifestyle
    Low Self-Esteem
    Anger
	CONS
	
	Overdose
	Death
	Suicide/Homicide
	Jail/Prison
	Hospitalized
	Homeless
	Divorce
	Bankruptcy
	Family/children
	Parental Rights
	Standing in Community

Short Term Pros & Benefits

Name: *John*　　　　　　　　Date: _____

1. **FROM THE BRAINSTORMING EXERCISE, LIST YOUR SHORT TERM PROS**
   (i.e. desire, ability, reasons and need to engage in your behavior).

   > *Energy*
   > *Stress*
   > *Focus*
   > *Social*
   > *Acceptance*

2. **WHAT OTHER WAYS COULD YOU DEAL WITH THESE SHORT TERM PROS?**

   > *Energy and Stress – play basketball, bike ride, lift weights*
   > *Focus - Keep a schedule, write out all appointments, plan my day*
   > *Social and Acceptance – go to support meetings, call a friend*

3. **WHAT WOULD BE SOME BENEFITS OF CHANGING YOUR BEHAVIOR?**

   > *I would feel better, regain the trust and respect I lost from my family and friends and be in control of my life.*

Short Term Pros & Benefits

Name:_____   Date: _____

1. **FROM THE BRAINSTORMING EXERCISE, LIST YOUR SHORT TERM PROS**
   (i.e. desire, ability, reasons and need to engage in your behavior).

2. **WHAT OTHER WAYS COULD YOU DEAL WITH THESE SHORT TERM PROS?**

3. **WHAT WOULD BE SOME BENEFITS OF CHANGING YOUR BEHAVIOR?**

Altered States Descriptor

It is human to seek altered states to give life purpose, meaning and fulfillment. Brain chemistry permits transient ecstasy or pleasure. Sustained ecstasy is neurophysiologically impossible. (*What does this mean*)?

Addictions and compulsive behaviors defy natural brain functioning, fabricating a sense of pleasure usually for a longer period of time and/or more intensively than what our brains can produce under normal circumstances.

The "crash" we experience after an addictive / compulsive episode is, in part, due to our bodies and brains attempting to compensate for the overload. (*What else is this called*)?

Natural highs are compatible with our brain functions. This is one reason we continue to feel good and do not experience a "crash" after a natural pleasure or after utilizing a healthy coping skill.

We rely on three distinct types of experiences to achieve feelings of well-being: *relaxation, excitement/arousal, and fantasy*.

- *Relaxation* **includes any activity that slows the body and mind down, such as meditating, bird watching, gardening, church, reading, walking, etc.**

- *Excitement/arousal* **is the opposite. It includes anything that speeds the body and mind up, such as competitive sports, running, skydiving, water/snow skiing, etc.**

- *Fantasy* **is using your imagination, and/or getting physical sensations from watching others perform an activity, such as watching sports, watching movies, reading, etc.**

Different addictions and compulsive behaviors fit into the same categories:

- *Relaxation*: **alcohol, heroin, tranquilizers, Quaaludes, barbiturates, etc.**

- *Excitement/arousal:* **gambling, sexual addiction, cocaine, amphetamines, etc.**

- *Fantasy:* **LSD, peyote, psylicybin mushrooms, marijuana, etc.**

Name: *John* _____   Date: _____

ACTIVITIES / BEHAVIORS TO HELP AVOID OR ALTER BEHAVIOR.
(Check the activities/behaviors that you would be interested in trying)

- ✔ H.A.L.T. (Hungry –eat, Angry –do something physical, Lonely –call a friend, Tired – sleep, rest).
- Read information
- Review your exercises from group
- ✔ Go to a support meeting
- Meet new friends
- Focus on doing a good job
- ✔ Do something to please family or friends
- Share your opinion and feelings
- Participate in lively discussions
- ✔ Complete a task
- Go people watching
- Express your affection
- Have coffee with a friend
- Anticipate a future event
- Go sun bathing / tanning
- Play with animals
- ✔ Plan a special project
- Learn a new skill
- ✔ Acquire knowledge
- Have a good night sleep
- Have time to do something you like
- Talk and listen to your loved ones
- Feel relaxed
- ✔ Be with a loved one
- Do something to make you feel attractive
- Breath fresh air
- Have pleasant thoughts about loved ones or friends
- Have sex
- Go out for lunch or dinner
- See or make good things happen to your family
- Pay someone a compliment
- Drive with care and caution
- Express yourself clearly
- ✔ Eat a good and special meal
- Wear something special
- ✔ Experience peace and quiet
- Laugh
- See beautiful things

Teach / coach / mentor
✔ **Participate in strenuous activities**
Go to a play or concert
Contribute your time
Camp in the mountains
✔ **Go fishing or hiking**
Do volunteer work
Ride a bus / train –go somewhere different
Buy something for yourself
Work on a problem
Assert yourself
Be at a special ceremony
Dine with friends
Participate in a church activity
✔ **Make something from different materials**
Dance
Go places where there are happy people
Listen to beautiful sounds of nature (wind, waterfall, waves)
Go on a date
Compete in a sports event
Give a present
Write a letter
Bath or take a shower
Attend a meeting or lecture
Attend a cultural activity
Cook a special meal
Receive advice from a mentor or friend
Take pictures or photographs
Look for interesting things (rocks, driftwood)
✔ **Watch a sunset / sunrise / cloud formation**
Invite friends to visit
Hear a funny story or joke
✔ **Watch a video**
Join and participate in a club
Go swimming
Play an outdoor game
✔ **Listen to music**
Read something special / go to the library
Use the computer
Watch a fire
Take a tour
Bake
Other Activities / Behaviors:
Play basketball, ride bike, lift weights

Altered States Categorizer

Name: _John_   Date: _____

(List the activities / behaviors you selected from the preceding 2 pages next to the appropriate category listed below):

PHYSICAL ACTIVITIES: *Play basketball, ride bike, and lift weights.*

RELAXATION ACTIVITIES: *Plan a special project, be with a loved one, eat a special meal, fishing, make something, watch a video, and listen to music.*

COGNITIVE / AFFIRMATIONS: *Go to a support meeting, do something to please family or friends, and acquire knowledge.*

ART / CREATIVE / AESTHETIC: *Watch a sunrise or sunset.*

MEDITATION / PRAYER: *Experience peace and quiet; hike.*

LIST BELOW THE ACTIVITIES / BEHAVIORS YOU WOULD BE WILLING TO ENGAGE IN TO HELP YOU ALTER / AVOID YOUR BEHAVIOR:

Play basketball, ride bike, lift weights, go for a hike, plan a special project, watch a video, listen to music, and go to a support meeting.

Menu of Alternatives

Name: _____   Date: _____

ACTIVITIES / BEHAVIORS TO HELP AVOID OR ALTER BEHAVIOR.
(Check the activities/behaviors that you would be interested in trying)

H.A.L.T. (Hungry –eat, Angry –do something physical, Lonely –call a friend, Tired –sleep, rest).
Read information
Review your exercises from group
Go to a support meeting
Meet new friends
Focus on doing a good job
Do something to please family or friends
Share your opinion and feelings
Participate in lively discussions
Complete a task
Go people watching
Express your affection
Have coffee with a friend
Anticipate a future event
Go sun bathing / tanning
Play with animals
Plan a special project
Learn a new skill
Acquire knowledge
Have a good night sleep
Have time to do something you like
Talk and listen to your loved ones
Feel relaxed
Be with a loved one
Do something to make you feel attractive
Breathe fresh air
Have pleasant thoughts about loved ones or friends
Have sex
Go out for lunch or dinner
See or make good things happen to your family
Pay someone a compliment
Drive with care and caution
Express yourself clearly
Eat a good and special meal
Wear something special
Experience peace and quiet
Laugh
See beautiful things

Teach / coach / mentor
Participate in strenuous activities
Go to a play or concert
Contribute your time
Camp in the mountains
Go fishing or hiking
Do volunteer work
Ride a bus / train –go somewhere different
Buy something for yourself
Work on a problem
Assert yourself
Be at a special ceremony
Dine with friends
Participate in a church activity
Make something from different materials
Dance
Go places where there are happy people
Listen to beautiful sounds of nature (wind, waterfall, waves)
Go on a date
Compete in a sports event
Give a present
Write a letter
Bath or take a shower
Attend a meeting or lecture
Attend a cultural activity
Cook a special meal
Receive advice from a mentor or friend
Take pictures or photographs
Look for interesting things (rocks, driftwood)
Watch a sunset / sunrise / cloud formation
Invite friends to visit
Hear a funny story or joke
Watch a video
Join and participate in a club
Go swimming
Play an outdoor game
Listen to music
Read something special / go to the library
Use the computer
Watch a fire
Take a tour
Bake
Other Activities / Behaviors:

_____

_____

_____

Altered States Categorizer

Name: _____   Date: _____

(List the activities / behaviors you selected from the preceding 2 pages next to the appropriate category listed below):

PHYSICAL ACTIVITIES:

RELAXATION ACTIVITIES:

COGNITIVE / AFFIRMATIONS:

ART / CREATIVE / AESTHETIC:

MEDITATION / PRAYER:

LIST BELOW THE ACTIVITIES / BEHAVIORS YOU WOULD BE WILLING TO ENGAGE IN TO HELP YOU ALTER / AVOID YOUR BEHAVIOR:

SESSION FOUR: Values

Time Allowed: 90 minutes

Rationale

"The further in the shift occurs, the more sweeping will be the resulting change." This is based on Rokeach's Values model (1973), <u>The Nature of Human Values.</u> Values are those elements from within one's self that are really important and have a preference focus. Values are standards and qualities that help establish a purpose and direction. When one identifies values, one has the power to exert considerable force, influencing and directing one's behavior. One gains insight about their decision-making processes. Decisions that are consistent with one's values provide a sense of satisfaction, enhanced energy and self-esteem. Values help determine one's philosophy and act as guidelines to determine the quality of one's life.

"To trigger change, one would seek to increase the discrepancy between status and goal, where I see myself being and where I want to be." This is based on Kanfer's (1986) Self Regulation Theory.

Purpose

Clarify, identify and affirm the client values. Build intrinsic desire for change. Increase the client's awareness of the discrepancy between behavior and values. Heighten problem recognition and the desire for change, increase the client's own arguments for change.

Facilitator Mind Set

The facilitator engages clients by utilizing an empathetic style of reflective listening, accurate understanding, acceptance and respect. Keep it safe; everything you do is purposeful to enhance motivation and commitment. Roll with resistance. Ambivalence is normal. Remember, every person's change process is an individual process and occurs at his/her own pace. Trust the process (don't need to push it). The exercises will elicit change talk. Listen to and affirm change talk. Let clients hear themselves. Know when to be quiet. Don't debate, argue or confront. Confrontation is a goal, not a strategy. "Clients will come face to face with a difficult reality in a way that will change them" (Miller).

Materials needed for this session

Supplies: folders, pens, clipboards, dry erase board and dry erase pen.

Client Handouts:
>   Values Exercises Instructions (1 & 2)
>   List of Values
>   Prioritized Values - Worksheet
>   Homework – Exercise 2

Other Paperwork
>   Client Sign In sheet
>   Roster/tracking sheet
>   Vision homework – if client will be completing his/her third session.
>   **Post Assessment Handouts – 16-18 and Handout 19 Client Satisfaction Survey** for clients presenting their Vision in group.
>   **Handouts 21** (Quotes) & **22** (Poem), for clients who have completed the Motivation Group.

Procedures

1. Clients sign in and the facilitator checks the roster. (Sign in sheet and Rosters**, pg. 94-95).**

2. The process for the check in is as follows: Check in. Name. Date of last time they engaged in their behavior. Why they are in the group. Identify other groups they may be attending and the counselors they see. Identify how they are feeling and how they are taking care of themselves. Check in with them to verify if they have done their homework. Notify those who are going to receive their vision homework to stay after group. Check in with the members who are completing the group to see if they have done their Vision Homework.

    If they have not completed their Vision homework, they will do the Vision exercise **(Handout 20, pg.97-98)** in the final group session as part of their exercise. They will stay after group to complete the **Post-Assessment** exercises and compare their Pre and Post Assessment exercises with the facilitator. (Their **Pre Assessment exercises Handouts 5-7**, are in their folders). Once they have completed the entire group, the facilitator will disperse **Handouts 21-** Quotes and **22** - Poem, (**pg. 85-86**). These two handouts are given as a form of closure and to say good-bye to each client.

3. Put the quote on the board. Ask them to reflect on the quote that is about change. Ask how they relate to the quote in terms of changes they have made in their life, now or in their past.

4. Review homework.

5. Distribute the **Post Assessment** exercises and **Client Satisfaction Survey** to those presenting their vision and completing the group. The **Post Assessment** exercises are **Handouts 16-18** and **Handout 19, Client Satisfaction Survey**. All the handouts are to be completed in the group session.

6. Distribute the make-up exercise to clients who have already completed this group exercise in a prior group session.

7. The facilitator will start the session by having a short discussion on values, starting with the question "What are values"? Summarize the client input. The facilitator will emphasize: that values are neither right nor wrong; values change over time; there are core values we learn growing up; values we adopt throughout our life experiences; and values that we still want to achieve.

    The facilitator will discuss the concept of discrepancies between values and behavior. Utilizing the following example, the facilitator demonstrates this. Example*: A person is offered a job that requires frequent travel. The person decides to accept the job without considering their number 1 value of family. Ask how this person might feel as a result of this decision?* The discrepancy is the struggle between one's value and one's decision. What would make the decision congruent for this person?

8. The facilitator will introduce the values exercise, reminding the clients that the exercise may produce vulnerable feelings. To insure safety, there will not be any cross talk or debate about what individuals present. They will be asked to read their exercise out loud. The facilitator will inform them that they will be asked two questions when they have completed their presentation of their values exercise. The facilitator will also inform them that they may experience some discomfort in answering the questions. The facilitator will talk about "this discomfort" (discrepancy), after everyone has presented their exercise.

9. Give clients handout packet
    • Values Exercise Instructions: Handout 13 - (pg. 63).
    • Values Exercise 1 - Handout 14 - List of Values (pg. 66 & p.67)
    • Prioritized Values Worksheet - Handout 14 (pg.69).

10. The facilitator will explain that this exercise is a four-step process. The clients will begin by reviewing the two-page list of values and they will check off all the values that are most important to them. When they have completed the first step, they will star their top six values. The third step is to have them prioritize the top six values they have selected.

11. The fourth step is to use the worksheet to list the six prioritized values. On the bottom half of the worksheet, the clients will define their values. The facilitator will explain that the definitions are very important because they emphasize the specific meaning for each individual. Although values may be similar, how people define them is what makes them unique.

12. The facilitator will explain to the clients to read out loud their six prioritized values and definitions, with no discussion. The facilitator will remind the clients that they will be asked two questions after they present their exercise. The facilitator will ask the following questions: **1)** *How has your behavior negatively impacted each of your values?* And **2)** *Which of your values support your behavior?* *The facilitator will instruct them to respond to the questions by examining each of their values and definitions individually* (i.e. clients can't say "all of them").

13. The facilitator will thank each client, when they finish reading their values **AND** after they respond to questions posed.

14. The facilitator will acknowledge that the clients may have felt some discomfort when describing the impact their behavior has had on their values. This discomfort occurs when their behavior is not congruent with their values. This is **discrepancy**.

15. The facilitator explains that when one's behaviors are congruent with their values they often describe feelings of inner peace.

16. **Homework Handout 15 - Values Exercise 2 (p.71)**. The facilitator will have them write their top six values on the homework sheet. The clients will be asked to keep their values in mind throughout the next week. This exercise is designed to emphasize the potential changes in clients' behaviors as they integrate their values into their daily lives.

17. Remind them the homework will be reviewed the next week (bring it back).

18. Have the clients doing make-up exercise present their work in the group session.

19. Have the members who are completing their final session, present their vision. Have them read their summary page and then their vision.

20. Have all the clients turn in their exercises. The clients will fill out the **Group Summary** sheet (pg.96), while the facilitator makes copies of their exercises. The facilitator will return the original exercises back to the clients. Have the members put the originals back into the folders. The facilitator will collect the group summaries and folders as they leave.

21. The facilitator reviews the **Pre and Post Assessment** exercises with those clients who are completing their final session. The Pre-assessment exercises are in their folders. When a client completes their final session, they will receive their folder and a copy of the **Quotes (Handout 21)** and the **Poem (Handout22).**

22. The clients that need to complete the Vision Homework **(Handout 20 (pg. 97-98)** will remain after the group session to review the exercise with the facilitator. The clients will take out three exercises they have completed from their folder: **Areas of Impact** – (Part B), **Feelings** underlined, and the six **Values** they prioritized. From the exercises, the clients will complete the vision exercise summary sheet, **(pg 97).** The facilitator will review the direction under **Part B** of the Vision exercise for clients to complete at home.

Values Exercises Instructions

Name: _____   Date: _____

GROUP EXERCISE 1: Read through the two-page list of values and check off your most important values. From the values that you selected, star the top six. Now prioritize them, numbering your values one through six. On the worksheet, list your prioritized top six values, and define them.

HOMEWORK:

EXERCISE 2: List your six prioritized values and write any behaviors and/or activities you engaged in during the week, that support your values.

Exercise 1

List of Values

	✔	ACCEPTANCE	to fit in with others
		ACCURACY	to be correct in my opinions and actions
*	✔	ACHIEVEMENT	to accomplish and achieve
		ADVENTURE	to have new and exciting experiences
		ATTRACTIVENESS	to be physically attractive
		AUTHORITY	to be in charge of others
		BEAUTY	to appreciate beauty around me
		CARING	to take care of others
		COMFORT	to have a pleasant, enjoyable life
	✔	COMPASSION	to feel concern for others
		COMPLEXITY	to have a life full of variety and change
*	✔	CONTRIBUTION	to make a contribution that will endure
		COURTESY	to be polite and considerate to others
		CREATIVITY	to have new and original ideas
*	✔	DEPENDABILITY	to be reliable and trustworthy
		ECOLOGY	to live in harmony with the environment
*	✔	FAITHFULNESS	to be loyal and reliable in relationships
		FAME	to be known and recognized
	✔	FAMILY	to have a happy, loving family
		FLEXIBILITY	to adjust to new or unusual situations easily
		FORGIVENESS	to be forgiving of others
		FRIENDS	to have close, supportive friends
		FUN	to play and have fun
	✔	GENEROSITY	to give what I have to others
		GOD'S WILL	to seek and obey the will of God
	✔	GROWTH	to keep changing and growing
		HEALTH	to be physically well and healthy
		HELPFULNESS	to be helpful to others
		HONESTY	to be truthful and genuine
		HOPE	to maintain a positive and optimistic outlook
	✔	HUMILITY	to be modest and unassuming
		HUMOR	to see the humorous side of myself
	✔	INDEPENDENCE	to be free from dependence on others
		INDUSTRY	to work hard and well at my life tasks
		INNER PEACE	to experience personal peace
		NTIMACY	to share my innermost feelings with others
		JUSTICE	to promote equal and fair treatment for all

		KNOWLEDGE	to learn and possess valuable knowledge
	✔	LEISURE	to take time to relax and enjoy
		LOGIC	to live rationally and sensibly
		LOVED	to be loved by those close to me
		MODERATION	to avoid excesses and find a middle ground
	✔	MONOGAMY	to have one close, loving relationship
		ORDERLINESS	to have a life that is ordered and organized
		PLEASURE	to feel good
		POPULARITY	to be well-liked by many people
		POWER	to have control over others
	✔	RESPONSIBILITY	to make and carry out important decisions
		REALISM	to see and act realistically and practically
		RISK	to take risks and chances
		ROMANCE	to have intense, exciting love relationships
		SAFETY	to be safe and secure
		SELF-CONTROL	to be disciplined and govern my own actions
		SELF-ESTEEM	to like myself just as I am
*	✔	SELF-KNOWLEDGE	to have a honest understanding of myself
		SERVICE	to be of service to others
		SEXUALITY	to have an active and satisfying sex life
		SIMPLICITY	to live life simply, with minimal needs
	✔	STABILITY	to have a life that stays fairly consistent
		STRENGTH	to be physically strong
		SPIRITUALITY	to grow spiritually
	✔	TOLERANCE	to accept and respect those unlike myself
		TRADITION	to follow set patterns of the past
*	✔	VIRTUE	to live a morally pure and excellent life
		WEALTH	to have plenty of money
		WORLD PEACE	to work to promote peace in the world

LIST OTHER VALUES YOU MAY HAVE NOT LISTED:

_____

_____

_____

Exercise 1

List of Values

ACCEPTANCE	to fit in with others
ACCURACY	to be correct in my opinions and actions
ACHIEVEMENT	to accomplish and achieve
ADVENTURE	to have new and exciting experiences
ATTRACTIVENESS	to be physically attractive
AUTHORITY	to be in charge of others
BEAUTY	to appreciate beauty around me
CARING	to take care of others
COMFORT	to have a pleasant, enjoyable life
COMPASSION	to feel concern for others
COMPLEXITY	to have a life full of variety and change
CONTRIBUTION	to make a contribution that will endure
COURTESY	to be polite and considerate to others
CREATIVITY	to have new and original ideas
DEPENDABILITY	to be reliable and trustworthy
ECOLOGY	to live in harmony with the environment
FAITHFULNESS	to be loyal and reliable in relationships
FAME	to be known and recognized
FAMILY	to have a happy, loving family
FLEXIBILITY	to adjust to new or unusual situations easily
FORGIVENESS	to be forgiving of others
FRIENDS	to have close, supportive friends
FUN	to play and have fun
GENEROSITY	to give what I have to others
GOD'S WILL	to seek and obey the will of God
GROWTH	to keep changing and growing
HEALTH	to be physically well and healthy
HELPFULNESS	to be helpful to others
HONESTY	to be truthful and genuine
HOPE	to maintain a positive and optimistic outlook
HUMILITY	to be modest and unassuming
HUMOR	to see the humorous side of myself and the world
INDEPENDENCE	to be free from dependence on others
INDUSTRY	to work hard and well at my life tasks
INNER PEACE	to experience personal peace
INTIMACY	to share my innermost feelings with others
JUSTICE	to promote equal and fair treatment for all

KNOWLEDGE	to learn and possess valuable knowledge
LEISURE	to take time to relax and enjoy
LOGIC	to live rationally and sensibly
LOVED	to be loved by those close to me
MODERATION	to avoid excesses and find a middle ground
MONOGAMY	to have one close, loving relationship
ORDERLINESS	to have a life that is well-ordered and organized
PLEASURE	to feel good
POPULARITY	to be well-liked by many people
POWER	to have control over others
RESPONSIBILITY	to make and carry out important decisions
REALISM	to see and act realistically and practically
RISK	to take risks and chances
ROMANCE	to have intense, exciting love relationships
SAFETY	to be safe and secure
SELF-CONTROL	to be disciplined and govern my own actions
SELF-ESTEEM	to like myself just as I am
SELF-KNOWLEDGE	to have a honest understanding of myself
SERVICE	to be of service to others
SEXUALITY	to have an active and satisfying sex life
SIMPLICITY	to live life simply, with minimal needs
STABILITY	to have a life that stays fairly consistent
STRENGTH	to be physically strong
SPIRITUALITY	to grow spiritually
TOLERANCE	to accept and respect those unlike myself
TRADITION	to follow set patterns of the past
VIRTUE	to live a morally pure and excellent life
WEALTH	to have plenty of money
WORLD PEACE	to work to promote peace in the world

LIST OTHER VALUES YOU MAY HAVE NOT LISTED:

_____

_____

_____

_____

Worksheet

Name _John_   **Date** _____

HIGH PRIORITY VALUES

1. _achievement_

2. _contribution_

3. _dependability_

4. _faithfulness_

5. _self-knowledge_

6. _virtue_

DEFINE YOUR VALUES:

1. _To stick to my everyday planner, mental and on paper and complete anything that has to be completed._

2. _To give my best to help anyone who may be interested in my opinion or need what I have to give._

3. _When I say I'll be there I will. When I think I can do it, it will be done._

4. _I don't need to cheat to get more. I have everything I need._

5. _I know myself better than anyone._

6. _My virtue is located deep inside my self-knowledge. Now all I need is the combination._

Worksheet

Name _____   **Date** _____

HIGH PRIORITY VALUES

1. _____

2. _____

3. _____

4. _____

5. _____

6. _____

DEFINE YOUR VALUES:

1. _____

_____

2. _____

_____

3. _____

_____

4. _____

_____

5. _____

_____

6. _____

_____

Homework

Name *John*   Date _____

EXERCISE 2

List your six prioritized values and write any behaviors and/or activities you engaged in during the week, that support your values.

1. *achievement* – *Working on my projects at home.*

2. *contribution* – *Helping my neighbor move.*

3. *dependability* – *Going to group, work, meetings. Making all my appointments.*

4. *faithfulness* – *Being monogamous.*

5. *self-knowledge* – *Being honest with myself and my family.*

6. *virtue* – *Being aware of my values everyday.*

Homework

Name _____   Date _____

EXERCISE 2

List your six prioritized values and write any behaviors and/or activities you engaged in during the week, that support your values.

1. _____

2. _____

3. _____

4. _____

5. _____

6. _____

SESSION FIVE: Vision/Post Assessment
Time Allowed: 90 minutes

Rationale for this session
Creating a vision comes out of understanding who you are. Rediscovering who you are motivates change and inspires a new vision. With a fuller understanding of yourself, you can develop a renewed sense of going after what you really want. Creating your vision has to do with helping you reconnect with your own potential. Having a vision motivates you to be genuinely interested in a different path and reclaiming parts of yourself that you thought were lost.

Purpose
To reassess clients' commitment, confidence levels and motivation for change. Clients will confront their own arguments for change and come to terms with any discrepancies of status and goal. The vision will evoke the client's intentions to change and strengthen optimism that change is possible.

Facilitator Mind Set
The facilitator engages clients by utilizing an empathetic style of reflective listening, accurate understanding, acceptance and respect. Keep it safe; everything you do is purposeful to enhance motivation and commitment. Roll with resistance. Ambivalence is normal. Remember, every person's change process is an individual process and occurs at his/her own pace. Trust the process (don't need to push it). The exercises will elicit change talk. Listen to and affirm change talk. Let clients hear themselves. Know when to be quiet. Don't debate, argue or confront. Confrontation is a goal, not a strategy. "Clients will come face to face with a difficult reality in a way that will change them" (Miller).

Materials:
Supplies: folders, pens, clipboards, dry erase board and dry erase pen.

Client Handouts:
Vision handout if the client didn't complete it at home.
Post-Assessment packet:
Areas of Impact
Wheel of Change
Commitment rating
Client satisfaction Survey
Quotes and Poem

Procedures

1. Clients sign in and the facilitator checks the roster. (Sign in sheet and Rosters, **pg. 94-95).**

2. The process for the check in is as follows: Check in. Name. Date of last time they engaged in their behavior. Why they are in the group. Identify other groups they may be attending and the counselors they see. Identify how they are feeling and how they are taking care of themselves. Check in with them to verify if they have done their homework. Notify those who are going to receive their vision homework to stay after group.

3. Put the quote on the board. Ask them to reflect on the quote that is about change. Ask how they relate to the quote in terms of changes they have made in their life, now or in their past.

4. Review homework.

5. Before starting the group exercise, give those clients presenting their visions, the Post assessment packet which includes the **Handouts 16-19 Post Assessment Exercises and Client Satisfaction Survey (p.79-82)** to be completed during the group session. After they complete this packet they will wait for the rest of the group to finish their exercise for this session.

6. Upon completion of the group exercise, those clients completing the motivation group will present their visions. The facilitator will ask them to read their summary page first and then their vision (Handout 20 - Example pg. 83-84).

7. Have all the clients turn in their exercises. The clients will fill out the **Group Summary** sheet (**pg.96**), while the facilitator makes copies of their exercises. The facilitator will return the original exercises back to the clients. Have the members put the originals back into the folders. The facilitator will collect the group summaries and folders as they leave.

8. The facilitator reviews the **Pre and Post Assessment** exercises with those clients who have completed their final session. The Pre-assessment exercises are in their folders. (**Facilitator Note:** When comparing the Pre and Post Assessment exercises you may observe the following on client's Post Assessment exercises: (1) <u>Areas of Impact:</u> that the client identified more areas of impact and rated the level of impact higher. (2) <u>Wheel of</u>

<u>Change</u>: that the client moved towards a different stage of change and (3) <u>Commitment and Confidence Level</u>: that the client's commitment level may be higher and his/her confidence level may be lower. All these changes are related to the increase in client's awareness of the need for change and his/her sense of self-efficacy that change is possible

9. When a client has completed their final session, they will receive their folder and a copy of the **Quotes (Handout 21)** and the **Poem (Handout 22)** as a form of closure.

10. The clients that need to complete the Vision Homework **(Handout 20, pg. 97-98)** will remain after the group session to review the exercise with the facilitator. The clients will take out three exercises they have completed from their folder: **Areas of Impact** – (Part B), **Feelings** underlined, and the six **Values** they prioritized. From the exercises, the clients will complete the vision exercise summary sheet, **(pg 97).** The facilitator will review the direction under **Part B** of the Vision exercise for clients to complete at home.

11. The facilitator will complete the treatment plans of those clients who completed the motivation group (**Example Treatment Plan, pg. 87**).

Post Assessment Handouts (16-19)

Name: _John_ .   Date: _____

Areas of Impact Assessment (Part A)

On a scale of 1-4, with **1** being the *least* impacted, and **4** being the *most*, please circle the level of negative impact your behavior has had on the different areas of your life.

Relationships	1	2	3	④
Work	1	2	③	4
Financial	1	2	3	④
Legal	1	2	3	④
Family	1	②	3	4
Education	1	②	3	4
Community	1	②	3	4
Physical Health	1	2	③	4
Emotional Health	1	2	③	4
Spirituality	1	2	③	4
Hobbies/Interest	1	2	3	④
Social Life	1	2	③	4
Character/Morals/Values	1	②	3	4
Self-esteem	1	②	3	4

(Part B) List the areas *most impacted* (**3 or 4**) by your behavior, in order of importance.

1. *relationships*

2. *financial*

3. *legal*

4. *hobbies / interests*

5. *work*

6. *physical health*

7. *social life*

8. *emotional health*

9. *spirituality*

Prochaska-Diclemente's Wheel Of Change

Name: _John_   Date: _____

Please read the definition of each stage of change, written below, and shade in the area of the wheel that identifies where you are, in the process of changing your behavior.

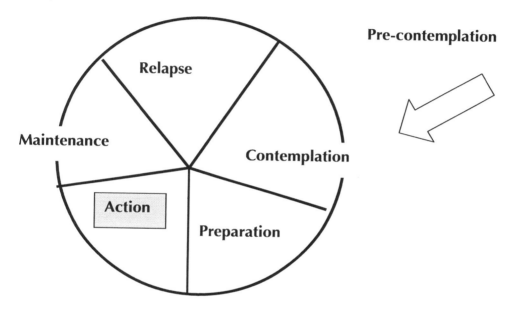

THE SIX STAGES OF CHANGE:

1. Pre-contemplation-**You do not think that your behavior is a problem.**

2. Contemplation-**You are considering the possibility of changing your behavior and at the same time rejecting the idea of change.**

3. Preparation-**You are leaning toward change, seriously considering no longer engaging in your behavior.**

4. Action-**You are taking steps to no longer engage in your behavior.**

5. Maintenance-**You are identifying and using strategies to prevent relapse and addressing other areas of your life.**

6. Relapse-**You are renewing the processes of contemplation, preparation and action and not giving up on your goal.**

Post-Assessment Exercise

Name: *John*   Date: _____

Self-Commitment Rating

At this moment, how important is it to you to change your behavior? How hard are you willing to work and how much are you willing to do? Answer this question by writing a number from 0-100 in the designated space below, using the following scale as a guide.

1	25	50	75	100
Not important at all	Less important than most other things I would like to achieve	About as important as most of the other things I would like to achieve	More important than most of the other things I would like to achieve	The most important thing in my life

Write your goal importance rating (from 0-100) here: 75%

Self-Confidence Rating (Do I believe I can succeed?)

How confident are you that you could make a change if you wanted to? Answer this question by writing a number from 0-100 in the designated space below, using the following scale as a guide.

0%	50%	100%
Not at all confident that I will achieve my goal	50-50 chance I will achieve my goal	Totally Confident I will Achieve my goal.

Write your confidence rating (from 0% - 100%) here: **100%**

Client Satisfaction Survey

CLIENT: _John_   DATE:_____

1. HAVE YOU MOVED FORWARD, BACKWARD, OR STAYED THE SAME, REGARDING YOUR ASSESSMENT OF THE NEED TO CHANGE YOUR BEHAVIOR, SINCE STARTING THIS GROUP. **(Please describe):**

   Due to the fact my attitude toward sobriety is much more positive, I have moved forward.

2. HOW USEFUL WERE THESE SELF – ASSESSMENT EXERCISES TO YOU? **(In what way):**

   They were put together very clearly. I feel much more comfort in explaining my deepest hard to find thoughts.

3. NAME TWO THINGS YOU LEARNED ABOUT YOURSELF?

   1. My will power is quite amazing.
   2. I don't have to use to be me.

4. DID YOU FEEL UNDERSTOOD, LISTENED TOO AND RESPECTED BY THIS COUNSELOR? **And were your treatment needs being addressed? (Please Describe)**

   Yes, I never felt looked down upon or talked down to. I'm clearer about the steps I know I need to take.

Post/Assessment Handouts (16-19)

Name: _____   Date: _____

Areas of Impact Assessment (Part A)

On a scale of **1-4,** with **1** being the *least* impacted**,** and **4** being the *most*, please circle the level of negative impact your behavior has had on the different areas of your life.

Relationships	1	2	3	4
Work	1	2	3	4
Financial	1	2	3	4
Legal	1	2	3	4
Family	1	2	3	4
Education	1	2	3	4
Community	1	2	3	4
Physical Health	1	2	3	4
Emotional Health	1	2	3	4
Spirituality	1	2	3	4
Hobbies/Interest	1	2	3	4
Social Life	1	2	3	4
Character/Morals/Values	1	2	3	4
Self-esteem	1	2	3	4

(Part B) List the areas *most impacted* (3 or 4) by your behavior, in order of importance.

1.

2.

3.

4.

5.

6.

7.

8.

Prochaska-Diclemente's Wheel Of Change

Name:_____   Date:_____

Please read the definition of each stage of change, written below, and shade in the area of the wheel that identifies where you are, in the process of changing your behavior.

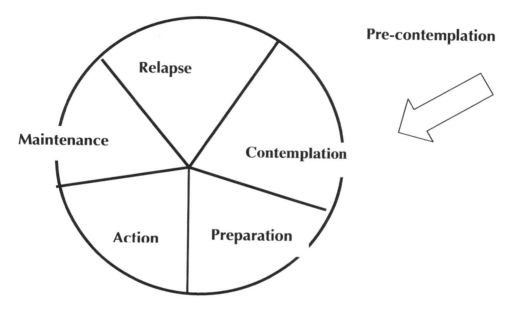

THE SIX STAGES OF CHANGE:

1. Pre-contemplation-**You do not think that your behavior is a problem.**

2. Contemplation-**You are considering the possibility of changing your behavior and at the same time rejecting the idea of change.**

3. Preparation-**You are leaning toward change, seriously considering no longer engaging in your behavior.**

4. Action-**You are taking steps to no longer engage in your behavior.**

5. Maintenance-**You are identifying and using strategies to prevent relapse and addressing other areas of your life.**

6. Relapse-**You are renewing the processes of contemplation, preparation and action and not giving up on your goal.**

Post-Assessment Exercise

Name: _____   Date: _____

Self-Commitment Rating

At this moment, how important is it to you to change your behavior? How hard are you willing to work and how much are you willing to do? Answer this question by writing a number from 0-100 in the designated space below, using the following scale as a guide.

1	25	50	75	100
Not important at all	Less important than most other things I would like to achieve	About as important as most of the other things I would like to achieve	More important than most of the other things I would like to achieve	The most important thing in my life

Write your goal importance rating (from 0-100) here: _____

Self-Confidence Rating (Do I believe I can succeed?)

How confident are you that you could make a change if you wanted to? Answer this question by writing a number from 0-100 in the designated space below, using the following scale as a guide.

0%	50%	100%
Not at all confident that I will achieve my goal	50-50 chance I will achieve my goal	Totally Confident I will Achieve my goal.

Write your confidence rating (from 0% - 100%) here: _____

Client Satisfaction Survey

Client: _____   Date:_____

1. **HAVE YOU MOVED FORWARD, BACKWARD, OR STAYED THE SAME, REGARDING YOUR ASSESSMENT OF THE NEED TO CHANGE YOUR BEHAVIOR, SINCE STARTING THIS GROUP. (Please describe):**

2. **HOW USEFUL WERE THESE SELF – ASSESSMENT EXERCISES TO YOU? (In what way?):**

3. **NAME TWO THINGS YOU LEARNED ABOUT YOURSELF?**

4. **DID YOU FEEL UNDERSTOOD, LISTENED TOO AND RESPECTED BY THIS COUNSELOR? And were your treatment needs being addressed? (Please Describe)**

82

Vision Exercise Summary Page

You are now coming to the end of the Motivation Group. To make a bridge from this Motivation Group to your next step, you will create a vision of the improvements or changes you hope will occur in the different areas of your life as a result of your commitment to and eventual achievement of your goal.

PART A. Please utilize the information from the exercises you have completed in group, and list the following information about yourself.

MOST IMPORTANT AREAS OF IMPACT:

Relationships
Character, morals and values
Emotional health
Hobbies / interests
Social life

FEELINGS DURING FIRST CONTACT:

vulnerable	satisfied	mad
embarrassed	worried	relaxed
powerlessness	anxious	relief
happy	guilty	nervous

VALUES:

Achievement	contribution
Dependability	faithfulness
Self-knowledge	virtue

PART B. On the following page, write several paragraphs describing the improvements or changes you are hoping to make over the next 3-6 months.

- Focus on the <u>Areas of Impact</u> you identified and prioritized, as being most impacted by your behavior.
- Add to your paragraph how you will feel when you make those improvements.
- Describe which of your values will support those changes and improvements.
- Use your imagination and don't limit or edit yourself.

Name: _John_   Date: _____

VISION

Within the next few months I hope to reduce my drinking to never. I know myself and it is definitely going to be a challenge, given the fact that all my friends drink when they get together. I plan on talking to them and explain that I have a problem and that I am going to need their help. I know that when I accomplish sobriety, I will be so proud of myself, but I will have to remind myself on a daily basis how long it has taken me to get here. And if I back track I will have to endure all of this pain all over again.

I think that the value of achievement will help me through this because the word means that I worked towards something and I have!

QUOTES

"What we call the beginning is often the end,
And to make our end is to make a beginning.
The end is where we start from."

T. S. Eliot

"I have always known that at last I would take this road,
but yesterday I did not know it would be today."

Narihira

"I can discard that which is unfitting and keep that which proved fitting,
and invent something new for that which I discarded."

Virginia Satir

"One change already influences other parts,
that means we can start anywhere."

Virginia Satir

POTENTIAL

It is something we can see in others,

If we see.

It is something we can feel in others,

If we feel.

It is something we can touch in others,

If we touch.

It is something we all have,

An inside desire to be more.

An energy so powerful, so human

It propels our growth.

Before it is kinetic,

Before there is change,

Our potential needs to be realized.

If we realize.

Ann Fields

Completed Treatment Plan

Name: _John_   Date:_ 6/02/03 _

GROUP: MOTIVATION GROUP
GOAL: To increase awareness of risks, level of self-efficacy and intrinsic desire for change.

Objective	Activity	Responsible Party	Frequency	Date Completed
A. Taking steps to reduce and/or no longer engage in your behavior.	1. Self-reports last time engaged in behavior.	Client	1x/wk	**6/30/03**
B. To assess stage of change, impact of behavior and level of commitment and confidence to making changes in your behavior.	2. Attend orientation prior to entering motivation group. Complete all pre-assessment exercises.	Client	1x	**6/2/03**
C. To increase awareness of risks of behavior and level of self-efficacy to change.	3. Attend all four motivation group sessions. Complete all group exercises and homework assignments.	Client	4x	**6/30/03**
D. To reassess stages of change and commitment and confidence levels to making changes in your behavior and create a vision of the hoped for changes and improvements in the different areas of your life.	4. Complete post-assessment exercises and present vision.	Client	1x	**6/30/03**
E. To collaborate and plan your next steps.	5. Contact referral counselor / provider after completing group.	Client	1x	**6/30/03**

John _____   _____
Client signature   **Counselor signature**

6/2/03 _____   **6/2/03** _____
Date   **Date**

COUNSELOR PREPARATION
AND ORGANIZATION

Be Organized.

This is a concrete way to track clients and the process of clients moving through the group exercises.

GROUP ROSTER:
- List new client's names on to the roster.
- Attach new member's treatment plan at the back of the roster.
- Place the initial of the exercise completed, under the correct date, next to each client's name. (O – orientation, P- pros & cons, V- values, F- feelings, VS - vision).
- Place a (/) for excused or (x) for no show, under the correct date, next to the client's name who did not come to group.
- Write VS and Completed, under the correct date, next to the client's names who presented their visions and completed the post-assessment exercises.

COUNSELOR ORIENTATION FOLDER:
Copies of the following Handouts:
- Orientation Sign-in sheet.
- Group Norms
- Facilitator Philosophy (Labels and Reactance)
- Freedom …
- Purpose of Group

Pre-Assessment Handouts:
- Areas of Impact
- Stages of Change
- Self-Commitment rating and Confidence rating
- Agency Treatment Plan
- Group Summary / Sign - out
- Folders – for new clients

Counselor Group Folder divided into three parts. The front part is used in group, the middle is used for group preparation and the end is for client's completed work
    Front: utilized in group:
- Quotes; to write on the board.
- Group check-in format; to write on the board.
- Client's Sign-in sheet.
- Group Roster, with attached treatment plans.
- Client's exercises, for the day.
- Client's Summary - sign-out sheet.

    Middle:
- A colored paper labeled Originals.
  Keep one original copy, of all the exercises, behind this paper.
  This way the counselor can easily find the exercises that need to be copied when he/she is preparing for the next group.

End:
- Clients completed copies of the exercises.
- Place six different colored pieces of paper in the back of your folder.
- Label them with the names of each of the exercises;
- Pros & Cons, Feelings, Values, Vision / Post assessment exercises, and Orientation / Pre assessment exercises.

Under each of these labeled colored papers is where you keep the copies of your client's completed exercises. (The original completed exercises are kept in the client's folders).

These copies are kept until the clients have completed the motivation group and received his/her folder.

Group Preparation:
Take a look at the roster to determine which exercise the majority of the group needs to complete.
> Count the number of clients who will be doing the group exercise.
> Make the copies of the exercise needed for the next group.
> Flag the front copy of the exercises with a sticky labeled _____ group exercise.

Take a look at the roster to see which client's need to do a make-up group exercise due to an absence.
> Make a copy of that exercise and flag the front of it with a sticky labeled with their name.

Take a look at the roster and see which clients have completed two exercises, do not include O - orientation.
> These clients will be receiving their vision exercise as homework, in the next group.
> Make copies of the vision exercise and flag them with a sticky labeled with their names.

Take a look at the roster to see which clients have completed all three exercises (P, V, F) and will be presenting their vision.
> Make copies of the Post-assessment exercises they need to complete in their final group; and flag the copies with a sticky labeled with their names.

At a glance - Counselor reminders: (*Example Roster Handout p.91*)
Flag the front of the group roster with the following:
- Label a sticky with the names of the clients receiving their vision homework.
- Label a sticky with the names of the clients presenting their vision.
- Label a sticky with individuals doing make-up exercises and the names of their exercises.
- Label a sticky with the name of the group exercise.
- Label a sticky with the homework exercise to be reviewed or handed in to the group counselor.

Group Roster Example

LIST TOPICS HERE ↓

VISION HOMEWORK	VISION
CORY	STEVE

O = Orientation
F = Feeling
P = Pros and Cons
V = Values
VS = Vision/Post Assessment

Name ↓ Date →	Orientation 6/2	Feelings 6/9	Pros & Cons 6/16	Values 6/23	Pros & Cons 6/30	Feelings 7/7	Values 7/14	Feelings 7/21	Pros & Cons 7/28	Values 8/4
John	O	F	P	V	VS					
Howard		O	P	V	F	/	VS			
Rebecca		O	X	V	P	/	F	VS		
Ruth			O	/	P	F	V	VS		
Theresa					O	F	V	/	X	
Dean					O	/	X			
Steve						O	V	F	P	
Cory						O	/	F	P	
Dan							O	F	/	
Jacen								O	P	

PROS & CONS	HOMEWORK

GROUP EXERCISE	VALUES

Absence/=excused x= no show

FORMS

Group Roster Example

LIST TOPICS HERE ↓

O= Orientation F = Feeling P = Pros and Cons V = Values VS = Vision/Post Assessment	Orientation	Feelings	Pros & Cons	Values	Pros & Cons	Feelings	Values	Feelings	Pros & Cons	Values									
Date → **Name ↓**	6/2	6/9	6/16	6/23	6/30	7/7	7/14	7/21	7/28	8/4									
John	O	F	P	V	VS														
Howard		O	P	V	F	/	VS												
Rebecca		O	X	V	P	/	F	VS											
Ruth			O	/	P	F	V	VS											
Theresa					O	F	V	/	X										
Dean					O	/	X												
Steve						O	V	F	P										
Cory						O	/	F	P										
Dan							O	F	/										
Jacen								O	P										

Absence/=excused x= no show

Group Roster

LIST TOPICS HERE ↓

O= Orientation F=Feelings P= Pros and cons V= Values VS= Vision /post assessment																					
Name ↓ Date →																					

Absence /=excused x= no show

Group Sign-In

Date _____   Counselor _____

NAME	DATE LAST ENGAGED IN BEHAVIOR	CURRENT MOOD

Group Summary (Client Weekly Update)

GROUP: _____

Facilitator: _____ **Date:** _____

Client's Name: _____**Group Time:** _____

Right now I'm feeling:

The topic of group today was:

What I learned about myself in this session:

How I'm feeling about group now:

_____

Counselor Notes:

Facilitator Signature: _____ Date: _____

Vision Exercise Summary Page

You are now coming to the end of the Motivation Group. To make a bridge from this Motivation Group to your next step, you will create a vision of the improvements or changes you hope will occur in the different areas of your life as a result of your commitment to and eventual achievement of your goal.

PART A. Please utilize the information from the exercises you have completed in group, and list the following information about yourself.

MOST IMPORTANT AREAS OF IMPACT:

FEELINGS DURING FIRST CONTACT:

VALUES:

PART B. On the following page, write several paragraphs describing the improvements or changes you are hoping to make over the next 3-6 months.

- Focus on the Areas of Impact you identified and prioritized, as being most impacted by your behavior.
- Add to your paragraph how you will feel when you make those improvements.
- Describe which of your values support those changes and improvements.
- Use your imagination and don't limit or edit yourself.

Name: _____   **Date:** _____

VISION

Bibliography

Bem, D.J. (1972) *Self-perception Theory.* In L. Berkowitz (Ed.), *Advances in experimental social psychology* (Vol. 6, pp. 1-62). New York: Academic Press.

Brehm, S. S., & Brehm, J. W. (1981) *Psychological Reactance: A theory of freedom and control.* New York: Academic Press.

DiClemente, C. C., & Prochaska, J. O. (1998). *Toward a comprehensive, transtheoretical model of change: Stages of change and addictive behaviors.* In W. R. Miller & N. Heather (Eds.) *Treating addictive behaviors* (2nd ed., pp.3-24) New York: Plenum Press.

Janis, I. L., & Mann, L. (1977) *Decision-making: A psychological analysis of conflict, choice, and commitment.* New York: Free Press.

Kanfer, F. H. (1986) *Implications of a self-regulation model of theory for treatment of addictive behaviors.* In W. R. Miller & N. Heather (Ed.), *Treating addictive behaviors* (pp. 29-47). New York: Plenum Press.

Miller, W. R. & Rollnick, S (1991) Motivational interviewing: *Preparing people to change addictive behaviors.* New York: Guilford Press.

Rogers, R. W. & Mewborn, C. R. (1976) Fear appeals and attitude change: Effects of a threat's noxiousness, probability of occurrence, and the efficacy of coping responses. *Journal of Personality & Social Psychology*, 34, 54-61.

Rokeach, M (Ed.). (1979) *Understanding human values.* New York: Macmillan.

About the Author

Ann E. Fields, MSE., CADC 111, CGAC 11
Trainer/Consultant

Ann Fields is originally from Dover, New Jersey. She currently resides in Vancouver, Washington. Ms. Fields holds a Bachelor of Arts degree in Psychology from Catawba College, Salisbury, North Carolina, a Bachelor of Science in Behavior Technology from the University of North Carolina, Greensboro, North Carolina and a Masters of Education degree from Western Oregon University, Monmouth, Or. Ms. Fields also has master-level certifications in substance abuse and gambling addictions.

She has also worked with William Miller in the original training cohort and was selected to participate in the first "Training for Trainers" program established by Miller in 1993. Ms. Fields is a registered MINT trainer (Motivational Interviewing Network of Trainers) in Washington and Oregon.

She has worked in the counseling field for more than 25 years and specializes in behavioral change. Throughout her career, she has been involved with innovative programs utilizing behaviorally oriented, research-based strategies and techniques to effect change with individuals, families, service providers, communities and large systems.

Ms. Fields provides specialized training and consultation to professional practitioners in a variety of practice arenas such as: mental health, medical social work, substance abuse, gambling addictions, child welfare, juvenile justice, corrections, family violence and family preservation services. As a guest lecturer for the Graduate School of Social Work, Portland State University, she has provided social work students with a foundation of basic concepts for utilizing motivational interviewing in their beginning social work practice, since 1998. She is a trainer for Daystar Education Associates and Portland State University's Continuing Education Program, both located in Portland, Oregon, a MIA-STEP Trainer for the Northwest Frontier ATTC and also a national trainer for PESI Health Care.

Made in the USA
Lexington, KY
12 August 2011